A Christology of Religions

A Christology of Religions

GERALD O'COLLINS, SJ

ORBIS BOOKS
Maryknoll, New York 10545

ORBIS BOOKS
Maryknoll, New York 10545

TOGETHER IN GOD'S MISSION OF MERCY

Founded in 1970, Orbis Books endeavors to publish works that enlighten the mind, nourish the spirit, and challenge the conscience. The publishing arm of the Maryknoll Fathers and Brothers, Orbis seeks to explore the global dimensions of the Christian faith and mission, to invite dialogue with diverse cultures and religious traditions, and to serve the cause of reconciliation and peace. The books published reflect the views of their authors and do not represent the official position of the Maryknoll Society. To learn more about Maryknoll and Orbis Books, please visit our website at www.maryknollsociety.org.

Library of Congress Cataloging-in-Publication Data

Names: O'Collins, Gerald, author.
Title: A Christology of religions / by Gerald O'Collins, SJ.
Description: Maryknoll : Orbis Books, 2018. | Includes bibliographical references and index. |
Identifiers: LCCN 2017054906 (print) | LCCN 2018005244 (ebook) | ISBN 9781608337477 (e-book) | ISBN 9781626982819 (pbk.)
Subjects: LCSH: Jesus Christ—Person and offices. | Christianity and other religions. | Theology of religions (Christian theology)
Classification: LCC BT203 (ebook) | LCC BT203 .O253 2018 (print) | DDC 232—dc23
LC record available at https://lccn.loc.gov/2017054906

Contents

Introduction

Through an article that appeared in 1959, Heinz Robert Schlette launched the term "theology of religions."[1] With contributions coming from around the world, this term and discipline have flourished in many courses, seminars, articles, and books, and have encouraged such spin-off terms and disciplines as comparative theology, intercultural theology, interfaith theology, interreligious theology, and the theology of interreligious dialogue. But, so far as I know, no one has proposed a "Christology of religions." Some have developed a "Christocentric" theology of religions, as distinguished from a "theocentric" or an "ecclesiocentric" theology of religions. But I have never come across a "Christology of religions."

How does a "Christology of religions" differ from a "Christocentric theology of religions"? After all, such a theology of religions reads the existence of those who follow "other" faiths (or none at all) through a Christological lens: that is to say, from the perspective of the person ("Christ in himself") and saving work ("Christ for us") of Jesus Christ. But modern Christocentric theologies of religion[2] do not generally operate on the basis of the full Christological picture. They largely ignore themes that belong to an integral Christology: the theology of the cross; the

---

1. H. R. Schlette, "Dogmatische Perspektiven im Hinblick auf die nichtchristchen Religionen," *Zeitschrift für Missionswissenschaft und Religionswissenschaft* 43 (1959), 275–89, at 289.

2. For a summary account of Christocentric theologies of religion, see Jacques Dupuis, *Christianity and the Religions: From Confrontation to Dialogue*, trans. Phillip Berryman (Maryknoll, NY: Orbis Books, 2002), 76–79.

universal impact of Christ's high-priestly ministry; the efficacy of his loving prayer for "the others"; and the mediation of his revelation (and not merely salvation) and the corresponding faith accessible to the "others." My *Christology of Religions* will attend to these highly significant and necessary themes.

Incorporating these new themes into contemporary discussion could help break a certain stalemate that affects some contested areas in the theology of religions, at least as it has been developed by Roman Catholics: for instance, the debates on the value of "other religions" in mediating salvation. This situation has even led Catherine Cornille, herself a notable contributor, to propose a moratorium.[3]

I am a Catholic and will cite teaching from the Second Vatican Council (1962–65) and from John Paul II (pope 1978–2005). The two theologians with whom I engage most were both Catholics: Karl Rahner (1904–84) and Jacques Dupuis (1923–2004). Nevertheless, I present this book as a Christology of religions that is Christian rather than specifically Catholic. It takes up the thought of Anglicans and Protestants such as Karl Barth, David Brown, Ingolf Dalferth, Hans-Georg Gadamer, Mark Heim, John Polkinghorne, John V. Taylor, and Tom Torrance—not to mention Craig Koester, Andrew Lincoln, Joel Marcus, and other biblical scholars. Moreover, the works in Christology that I have published with Oxford University Press, as well as with Baylor University Press, Continuum, Eerdmans, Darton, Longman & Todd, and Paulist Press were addressed to and have been received by teachers and students of various Christian denominations. It is as a Christian rather than specifically as a Catholic that I have continued to elaborate a Christology that is, or at least should be, shared by all Christians. It is in the same spirit that I now write *A Christology of Religions*.

---

3. Catherine Cornille, "Soteriological Agnosticism and the Future of Catholic Theology of Interreligious Dialogue," in T. Merrigan and J. Friday (eds.), *The Past, Present, and Future of Theologies of Interreligious Dialogue* (Oxford: Oxford University Press, 2017), 201–15.

To clarify the differences between Dupuis and Rahner, I published an article, "Was Jacques Dupuis a Neo-Rahnerian?"[4] Then I discussed Rahner when evaluating the background for Vatican II's teaching on those who follow "other" faiths or none at all.[5] I also noted how, for some years, he used the language of "anonymous Christians" to describe the situation of those who had received God's grace but had not yet accepted the gospel and been baptized. Rahner dropped this terminology as less than fully helpful.[6] In this book, Chapter 2 illustrates how Rahner failed to reflect theologically on the priesthood of Christ—both in general and in its relationship to all human beings, including those who belong to "other" religions or to none at all.

I have written more on Dupuis.[7] But I wish to qualify and go beyond what he has written, as will be seen in Chapters 1, 2, 4, 5, and 6. Apropos of his difficulties with the Congregation for the Doctrine of the Faith and their 2000 declaration *Dominus Iesus* (the Lord Jesus), readers can consult Chapter 5 below; a chapter that I wrote for *On the Left Bank of the Tiber*, "The Dupuis Case"[8]; and *Do Not Stifle the Spirit: Conversations with Jacques Dupuis*.[9]

A Christology of religions not only gives shape to reflections on the "others" but also indicates the material to be dealt with. Through the incarnation, the Son of God assumed the human

---

4. *Asian Horizons* 7 (2013), 237–60; reprinted as "Jacques Dupuis and Karl Rahner," in Gerald O'Collins, *Christology: Origins, Developments, Debates* (Waco, TX: Baylor University Press, 2015), 131–41, 169–72.

5. Gerald O'Collins, *The Second Vatican Council on Other Religions* (Oxford: Oxford University Press, 2013), 11–12, 50– 58.

6. Ibid. 56–57.

7. See articles in the *Gregorianum* (2003), *Theological Studies* (2003 and 2013), and *Vidyajvoti* (2005), as well as Chapter 9 in *The Second Vatican Council on Other Religions*, 181–96. The four articles are fully listed in my final bibliography below.

8. Gerald O'Collins, *On the Left Bank of the Tiber* (Ballarat, AU: Connor Court, 2013), 213–51.

9. Gerard O'Connell, *Do Not Stifle the Spirit: Conversations with Jacques Dupuis* (Maryknoll, NY: Orbis Books, 2017).

condition, became part of created reality, and shared the (suffering) history of all human beings. He identified himself with the created world and human history. To be created and to be human entail being vulnerable. Christ's particular history of vulnerability, which ended with death by slow torture on a cross, became the context and means of God's self-revelation to everyone and offer of saving grace to all people (Chap. 1).

The saving work of Christ took a triple form, through his "office" as priest, prophet, and king or shepherd. His high-priestly intercession for all people has its special place in this book. Crucified, buried, risen from the dead, and ascended to the heavenly glory of God the Father, he continues to intercede for all people and to gather into unity "the children of God who have been scattered" (John 11:52). The priestly work of Christ, while widely neglected, requires a prominent place in any Christology of religions (Chap. 2).

More and more Western theologians have come to realize that there can be no Christology without an appropriate pneumatology. When we apply this conviction to world religions, the universal presence and activity of the Holy Spirit should feature with the universal, priestly presence and activity of the risen and glorified Christ. To communicate the divine revelation and salvation to all, the Spirit and Christ function inseparably in their aim to bring the human race and its universe home to the Father. A Christology of religions should be a pneumatology of religions, and that necessarily means a trinitarian theology of religions (Chap. 3).

Chapter 4 will shift the focus from Christology and pneumatology to relevant aspects of ecclesiology. How effective is the church's prayer of intercession for "the others," which is inspired by love and joined with the eternal intercession of Christ the high priest?

Chapter 5 picks up Christ's solidarity with all those who suffer, a solidarity embodied in his vision of the last judgment (Matt. 25:31–46) and his death on a cross between two criminals. In the light of this universal suffering, what possibilities for faith are open to those who remain "in good faith" and yet never have a chance of being baptized and entering the Christian community?

The teaching of Pope John Paul II went beyond the Second Vatican Council, which spoke of the "seeds of the Word" present everywhere and recognized in the cultural and religious traditions of "others" the active presence of the Holy Spirit. Chapter 6 investigates this mysterious presence of Christ and his Spirit in the beliefs, practices, and cults of others.

A seventh chapter will turn to the practical consequences for a Christology of religions. After developing some reflections in terms of a fourfold dialogue with "the others," this chapter will highlight some consequences for relations with Jews and Muslims.

The book concludes with an epilogue that sums up the new proposals this book advances. An integral Christology that embraces, for instance, the cross and the high priesthood of Jesus Christ should reshape the theology of religions and endorse a full-blown Christology of religions.

As a Christian, I use the terminology of Old Testament (OT) and New Testament (NT). Here "old" is understood as good and does not imply any supersessionism, or the view that the NT has rendered obsolete, replaced, and so superseded the OT. For the English translation of biblical texts, I usually follow the New Revised Standard Version. The translations of any documents from the Second Vatican Council are my own and made directly from the original Latin texts. I wish to express my warm thanks to Dr. William Burrows, a treasured friend, who provided advice and support in seeing this book through to publication. I also thank Dr. Jill Brennan O'Brien, acquisitions editor at Orbis Books, for her valuable questions and excellent suggestions. With great gratitude, this book is dedicated to the members, past and present, of Newman College, University of Melbourne.

Abbreviations

AAS	*Acta Apostolicae Sedis* (Register of the Apostolic See)
ABD	D. N. Freedman, ed., *Anchor Bible Dictionary*, 6 vols. (New York: Doubleday, 1992)
CSEL	Corpus scriptorum ecclesiasticorum latinorum
DzH	H. Denzinger and P. Hünermann, eds., *Enchiridion symbolorum, definitionum et declarationum,* English trans., 43rd ed. (San Francisco: Ignatius Press, 2012)
ND	J. Neuner and J. Dupuis, eds., *The Christian Faith*, 7th ed. (Bangalore: Theological Publications in India, 2001)
NRSV	New Revised Standard Version of the Bible (Washington, DC: National Council of the Churches of Christ, 1989)
NT	New Testament
OT	Old Testament
par(r.)	and parallel(s) in other Gospels
REB	Revised English Bible (Oxford and Cambridge: Oxford University Press and Cambridge University Press, 1989)
Tanner	N. P. Tanner, ed., *Decrees of the Ecumenical Councils*, 2 vols. (London: Burns & Oates, 1990)
TRE	G. Krause and G. Müller, eds., *Theologische Realenzyklopädie*, 36 vols. (Berlin: Walter de Gruyter, 1977–2004)

The following abbreviations are used for documents of Vatican II:

AG	*Ad Gentes* (Decree on the Church's Missionary Activity)

DH	*Dignitatis Humanae* (Declaration on Religious Liberty)
GS	*Gaudium et Spes* (Pastoral Constitution on the Church in the Modern World)
LG	*Lumen Gentium* (Dogmatic Constitution on the Church)
NA	*Nostra Aetate* (Declaration on the Relation of the Church to Non-Christian Religions)
SC	*Sacrosanctum Concilium* (Constitution on the Sacred Liturgy)

Other Vatican documents cited:

DI	*Dominus Iesus* (The Lord Jesus), declaration, 2000
DV	*Dominum et Vivificantem* (Lord and Giver of Life), encyclical, 1986
EE	*Ecclesia de Eucharistia* (The Church from the Eucharist), encyclical, 2002
MD	*Mediator Dei* (On the Sacred Liturgy), encyclical, 1947
RH	*Redemptor Hominis* (The Redeemer of the Human Person), encyclical, 1979
RM	*Redemptoris Missio* (The Mission of the Redeemer), encyclical, 1990

1

Incarnation as Caring for "the Others" and Sharing the Sufferings of All

At a certain point in the history of the cosmos and of the human race, God acted in a unique way through the once-and-for-all sending or coming of his only Son. The Word was "made flesh" (John 1:14) or "in-carnated" by assuming a complete human nature and not simply an external bodily form. The eternal Son of God "took flesh" from a human mother. Hence the person known as Jesus of Nazareth was and remains at once fully human and truly divine. His earthly history was the "enfleshed" story of the Son of God and no "mere" theophany or transitory appearance of God. This incarnated presence of the Word of God engaged him in a new, hitherto unheard of, manner with the history of all human beings and the whole created universe, transforming that history forever. Through the interrelationship of all people and all things, the whole of history has now become his incarnational narrative.[1]

---

1. On the incarnation see S. T. Davis, D. Kendall, and G. O'Collins (eds.), *The Incarnation: An Interdisciplinary Symposium on the Incarnation of the Son of God* (Oxford: Oxford University Press, 2002); G. O'Collins, *Incarnation* (London/New York: Continuum, 2002). It is curious that there is no specific article on "incarnation" in Francesca A. Murphy and Troy S. Stefano (eds.), *The Oxford Handbook of Christology* (Oxford: Oxford University Press, 2015).

Some enduringly valuable insights coming from St. Athanasius of Alexandria could prompt us to ask: what does the incarnation mean for all human beings and for the entire world? Athanasius saw creation and incarnation as together forming *one* act of divine self-bestowal. The creative Word (or Wisdom of God) is now the deifying Word. All creatures exist precisely by sharing the Word in the Holy Spirit and so participating in deification. As Athanasius put matters, "the Father creates and renews all things through the Word and in the Spirit" (*Letter to Serapion* 1.24).[2] This eternal commitment of God to all matter and all "flesh" obviously provides one context for examining the religious situation of those who follow "other" living faiths (or none at all). Because of the incarnation, the entire human race, along with the whole created world, is in the process of being divinely transformed.

For Athanasius, then, through the creation and incarnation God became deeply engaged with *the deification not only of Christian believers but also of all other human beings.* An Athanasian approach to the Christology of religions deserves to be developed. But I do not want to leave behind the particularity of the historical story. Hence what follows in this chapter attends to the public ministry that came in the aftermath of the conception and birth of Jesus of Nazareth. After examining Jesus' message for everyone and, above all, his love command, we move to the cross and its relevance for a Christology of religions and the final transformation of his relationship with all human beings.

The incarnation made possible the ministry of Jesus, which centered less on founding the church than on proclaiming the kingdom or saving rule of God already powerfully present among all people but not yet fully consummated. That preach-

---

2. See D. Edwards, "Incarnation and the Natural World: Explorations in the Tradition of Athanasius," in N. H. Gregersen, *Incarnation: On the Scope and Depth of Christology* (Minneapolis: Fortress Press, 2015), 157–76; see also R. Bauckham, "The Incarnation and the Cosmic Christ," in ibid., 25–57; J. Behr, "Saint Athanasius on 'Incarnation,'" in ibid., 79–98.

ing eventually led to his passion and death on a cross. He is remembered by Matthew as having declared that his mission was to reform Israel and call Jews back to God: "I was sent only to the lost sheep of the house of Israel" (Matt. 15:24; see 10:5–6). Here "only" did not mean "exclusively." The frontiers for his mission on earth were porous. While Jesus took his mission of salvation primarily to his fellow Jews, he also reached out to some we can call "outsiders." They prefigured the millions of people who today follow "other" religious faiths or none at all but receive revelation and salvation from Jesus, even if they do not explicitly know him and believe in him.[3]

Caring for Some Gentile Individuals and Groups

Perhaps Jesus' most striking encounter with an individual outsider was that with a woman living in Gentile territory, "the districts of Tyre and Sidon"—that is to say, beyond upper Galilee and in Phoenicia (Mark 7:24–30). Mark identifies her as Greek and Syro-Phoenician,[4] while Matthew calls her a "Canaanite" (Matt. 15:21–28). Clearly she was not Jewish. We know nothing of her religious beliefs and practices, either before her

---

3. On our access to the historical Jesus and the criteria that enable us to move back from the texts produced by the four evangelists, through the traditions, to some approximate account of the sayings and doings of Jesus, I presuppose what I have written in *Christology: A Biblical, Historical, and Systematic Study of Jesus*, 2nd ed. (Oxford: Oxford University Press, 2009), 44–54.

4. J. R. Donahue and D. J. Harrington comment: "A 'Greek' (used only here in Mark) does not [necessarily] mean someone who is ethnically Greek but can be used as a generic term for a non-Jew. It also suggests someone who had assimilated Greek culture and language" (*The Gospel of Mark* [Collegeville, MN: Liturgical Press, 2002], 233). On the story of the Syro-Phoenician woman, see M. G. Brett, *Decolonizing God: The Bible in the Tides of Empire* (Sheffield: Sheffield Phoenix Press, 2008), 143–44; D. A. Hagner, *Matthew 14–28* (Dallas: Word Books, 1995), 438–53; U. Luz, *Matthew 8–20* (Minneapolis: Fortress Press, 2001), 336–42; J. Marcus, *Mark 1–8* (New York: Doubleday, 1999), 461–71; J. P. Meier, *A Marginal Jew: Rethinking the Historical Jesus* (New York: Doubleday, 1994), 2:659–61, 674–76.

meeting with Jesus or later. Somehow she had heard of him and asked for help for her tormented daughter. The episode stands out for the harsh, even insulting, language directed to a sincere and suffering petitioner. It "portrays a Jesus who is unusually sensitive to his Jewish countrymen's claim to have salvation-historical privilege and unusually rude about the position of Gentiles: the Jews are God's children, and their needs come first; compared to them, non-Jews are just dogs."[5] But the episode also stands apart as being the *only example* in all four Gospels of (a) an exorcism performed at a distance, and (b) someone who won an argument with Jesus. In Matthew's version she prompted him into saying, "woman, great is your faith" (Matt. 15:28). A Gentile dared to ask him for a miracle, and he was willing to perform it—thus, he began breaking down the barriers that separated Jews and Gentiles. Even though she did not share in the special blessings of Jewish covenant with God and seemingly had enjoyed no previous contact with him, Jesus, according to Matthew, praised her "great faith."

The Gospels record further episodes in which Jesus responded to the needs of non-Jews, both specific individuals and groups. In Capernaum, a centurion, a non-Jewish military officer in charge of fifty to one hundred soldiers, appealed to Jesus for help when his son (*pais*, which could also be translated "servant") fell desperately ill (Matt. 8:5–13).[6] Apparently the centurion knew that, as a Jew, Jesus should not enter the house of a Gentile. But he was convinced that a word of command would be enough, since diseases obeyed Jesus just as soldiers obeyed their officers. Jesus was astonished at the way the centurion trusted his (Jesus') power to work the cure: "Truly I tell you, in no one in Israel have I found such faith" (Matt. 8:10). The faith of this Gentile outsider put Israel to shame,

---

5. Marcus, *Mark 1–8*, 470.
6. On the healing of the centurion's son, see D. A. Hagner, *Matthew 1–13* (Dallas: Word Books, 1993), 200–16; Luz, *Matthew 8–20*, 8–12; Meier, *A Marginal Jew*, 2:718–27, 763–72.

in the sense that his faith went beyond anything Jesus had so far experienced in his ministry to Jews, those who enjoyed the special revelation of God given through Abraham, Moses, the prophets, and various wisdom figures.

We are left in the dark about the religious practice of the centurion, and how God and then Jesus had become known to him. In Luke's version of the story, leaders of the Jewish community pleaded on behalf of the centurion: "he loves our nation, and it is he who built our synagogue for us" (Luke 7:1–10).[7] Whatever his state, Jesus did not invite him to join the ranks of his disciples but healed the boy with a simple word of command. Before doing so, he introduced the image of God's final banquet to warn what would happen at the end: "I tell you, many will come from the east and the west and will eat with Abraham, Isaac, and Jacob in the kingdom of heaven, while the heirs of the kingdom will be thrown into the outer darkness."[8] This, in the words of Ulrich Luz, is a "pointed threat rather than something irrevocable. It may well go back to Jesus."[9] Luz comments on how the faith of the centurion, as "the first member of the gentile church," signaled that the final gathering of the nations had already begun in the ministry of Jesus. Instead of streaming to Mount Zion and joining themselves to the institutions of Jewish faith and life (as Third Isaiah and other prophets had foretold), the Gentiles will find the goal of their pilgrimage in "the kingdom of heaven."[10]

---

7. John's Gospel also includes a similar story, about a "royal official" whose son was at the point of death and who "believed" that Jesus' word could bring a cure (John 4:46–54). Despite some differences, this healing story appears to be another version of what we read in Matthew and Luke.

8. This seems to have been a free-floating saying from Jesus. Originally Jesus may have intended to refer only to the final gathering of scattered Jews (see Luke 13:28–29). In Matthew's text the saying is applied to Gentiles coming from the four corners of the earth to share in the final banquet with the long-dead patriarchs of Israel.

9. Luz, *Matthew 9–20*, 9.

10. Ibid., 11.

Banquets in great households, including wedding banquets (Matt. 25:1–13), had obviously caught the imagination of Jesus and provided material to express the final banquet to come—a banquet at which righteous people from "the nations" would sit at the table with the patriarchs of Israel. Through such an image Jesus conveyed his desire to create a new people who would include Jews and non-Jews. In picturing the final gathering as a feast "for all peoples," Jesus probably drew as well on a passage from Isaiah: "the Lord of hosts will make for all peoples a feast of rich food" (Isa. 25:6–10, at v. 6). As Luz points out, in Jewish tradition the image of a banquet was already "closely connected with the coming age."[11]

We may be asking too much precision from Matthew's Gospel and, ultimately, from what Jesus said and meant. But should we characterize the centurion as "the first member of the Gentile church"? Like the Syro-Phoenician woman, he was not invited to become a disciple and simply returned home. Did he continue to live by the knowledge of God that had already been given to him, like the Ninevites after their encounter with Jonah when they were led to a massive moral conversion but not a religious conversion that could have joined them to Israel? What happened to the centurion may not have corresponded to what we could symbolize as his becoming "the first member of the Gentile church."

The exorcisms that featured prominently in the wonder-working activity of Jesus included a dramatic deliverance of a demoniac who seems to have been non-Jewish (Mark 5:1–20). Even if textual variants do not allow us to pinpoint the precise locality (Gerasa or Gadara), the area (the Decapolis) was Gentile. The non-Jewish identity of the man "is suggested by the presence of a herd of swine into which the demons flee."[12]

---

11. U. Luz, *Matthew 21–28* (Minneapolis: Fortress Press, 2005), 50.

12. M. A. Chancey, *The Myth of a Gentile Galilee* (Cambridge: Cambridge University Press, 2002), 178. A group of Hellenistic cities situated east of Galilee and Samaria, the Decapolis contained predominantly Gentile communities; see ibid., 130–43. On the Gentile identity of the

Without being asked to do so by anyone, Jesus liberated this Gentile outcast from his fearful condition and restored him to normal society. Jesus did not allow him to become a disciple, but rather sent him off with a commission: "Go home to your friends, and tell them how much the Lord has done for you, and what mercy he has shown you" (Mark 5:19).

Along with this exorcism and the healing of the Syro-Phoenician woman's daughter, Mark includes two further miraculous deeds that Jesus performed in Gentile territory: the restoration of hearing and speech to a deaf mute (Mark 7:31–37) and the feeding of the four thousand (Mark 8:1–10). In Mark's narrative, crowds followed Jesus and/or joined him on his journey through the predominantly Gentile area of the Decapolis (Mark 7:31). The deaf mute, since he apparently belonged to that area, was presumably a Gentile. His cure, at least the way Mark presents it, symbolized a new world being born for everyone—a world of plenitude and blessing "springing into existence" through Jesus.[13]

The crowds who followed Jesus were with him for three days and faced a long journey home. He miraculously multiplied some loaves and fish to feed them (Mark 8:1–10). Earlier Jesus had miraculously fed five thousand fellow Jews (Mark 6:36–44). Now in a separate episode in Mark's story he provided an abundance of food for a crowd who seem to have been Gentiles. The second feeding substantially parallels the first and shows Jesus supplying food for Gentiles, after having done so previously for Jews.[14]

A healing story, which includes an "outsider" and is found only in Luke's Gospel, is that of ten lepers being cleansed by

---

possessed man, see also Marcus, *Mark 1–8*, 342, 347, and 353; and Meier, *A Marginal Jew*, 2:650–53, 664–67.

13. Marcus, *Mark 1–8*, 472–81, at 481; see Meier, *A Marginal Jew*, 2:711–14, 758–59.

14. Unlike Marcus, *Mark 1–8*, 482–97, some scholars argue that the two feedings are only alternative versions of one and the same feeding miracle; see Meier, *A Marginal Jew*, 2:950–66, 1022–38, at 956–58.

Jesus (Luke 17:11–19).[15] One of them, who unlike the other nine was not a Jew but a Samaritan, returned, "praising God," "prostrating himself" at Jesus' feet, and "thanking him." Jesus said to the man whom he called a "stranger," "your faith has made you well (saved you)"—words that he also used with two Jews, a woman cured of a long-standing hemorrhage (Luke 8:48), and a blind beggar who received his sight (Luke 18:42). In all three cases the verb conveys an idea of the divine power at work to rescue someone from an evil force. Spiritual, as well as merely physical, "saving" or "making well" was involved. The Samaritan "saw" what his healing implied, came to faith, and received salvation. In this way Jesus blessed a person who was doubly an outcast, as a leper and a "foreigner."

Samaria had come into existence when the kingdom of Israel was destroyed by the Assyrians in 721 BCE. Sargon II deported the Israelites and replaced them with people from Babylon and elsewhere. The land was no longer called Israel but Samaria. The inhabitants were no longer Israelites but Samaritans, a people whose worship of the Lord did not correspond to what was considered appropriate (2 Kgs. 17:1–41). At the time of Jesus, Jews and Samaritans were not on speaking terms. In John's Gospel some Jews insult Jesus by alleging that he is a Samaritan and is possessed by a demon (John 8:48). Hostile Samaritans would harass pilgrims going to keep a feast in Jerusalem (Luke 9:51–56), since they considered the temple on Mount Gerizim and not on Mount Zion the primary place to worship God (John 4:20).[16]

Luke and John recall in different ways the caring openness Jesus showed to the Samaritans. A spectacular example came in the parable that bears the name of "the Good Samaritan." A Jewish priest and a Levite (one of those designated to be lay

---

15. See J. A. Fitzmyer, *The Gospel According to Luke X–XXIV* (New York: Doubleday, 1985), 1148–56; Meier, *A Marginal Jew*, 2:701–6.

16. Chancey, *The Myth of Gentile Galilee*, 153–54; see S. Freyne, "Galileans," *ABD*, 2:876–79; R. Frankel and S. Freyne, "Galilee," in ibid., 879–99.

associates of the priests) fail to stop for a wounded traveler. It is a Samaritan, an outsider hardly expected to have much sympathy for Jews, who generously helps the wounded man (Luke 10:29–37). Jesus himself was not only ready to meet Samaritans (John 4:4–42), but also, unlike other rabbis, he did not avoid speaking in public with a woman, and a Samaritan at that (John 4:9, 27). By delicately encountering someone who, after running through five husbands, was now living with another man, Jesus quickly turned her into a missionary for him. Through her testimony and their own personal experience, many of the Samaritans came to express faith in Jesus as "the Savior of the world" (John 4:42).[17] Whatever we decide about the historical status of the Samaritan interlude in the ministry of Jesus,[18] it is of a piece with what Luke tells us about Jesus' outreach to the Samaritan leper and Jesus' own picture of a Samaritan traveler as a role model for those ready to help people in terrible distress.

To sum up: Jesus preached a kingdom and performed miraculous deeds in ways that at times reached beyond the frontiers of racial and religious separations honored by devout Jews of his time. His preaching of the kingdom was not limited by those frontiers but could go beyond them to "foreigners." God's reign here and hereafter was for everyone.

A Message for Everyone

It is the content of Jesus' preaching that offers the clearest grounds for establishing his outreach to everyone. By and large, he proclaimed the kingdom of God only to audiences of Jews, but his message was for everyone. Even if at times his message was addressed to a Jewish audience precisely as Jewish (e.g. Mark 12:1–12), normally his words were directed to men

17. John Meier points out that this language of "Savior of the world" was "very much at home in the Greco-Roman world" (*A Marginal Jew*, 2:770).

18. See A. T. Lincoln, *The Gospel According to John* (London: Continuum, 2005), 167–82.

and women precisely as creatures of God. It was this universal appeal that conveyed a sense that the divine kingdom and its claim knew no frontiers. Let us see some examples.

First, in a controversy with certain Pharisees over divorce (Mark 10:1–12), Jesus dismissed as secondary and a concession to the people's sinfulness the Mosaic legislation that allowed divorce. In the light of the creation of humankind (Gen. 1:29; 2:24), he expressed his ideal for marriage and his opposition to divorce: "the original will of God in creating man and woman was that they should constitute 'one flesh' in an indissoluble union." Jesus envisioned a "restored creation in which unity and mutuality in marriage mirror God's original plan."[19] That, of course, was to develop into a teaching that concerned not merely Jews but all human beings.

Second, Jesus set about founding a new family or final community. Looking around at a group sitting near him, he solemnly declared: "Whoever does the will of God is my brother and sister and mother" (Mark 3:35). He did not specify as candidates for his new family "all those Jews who do the will of God." Any man or woman—read now Buddhist, Confucian, follower of a traditional religion, Hindu, Muslim, Sikh, agnostic, and so forth—who does what God wants qualifies for admission to this new community and becomes, whether he or she knows it or not, truly related to Jesus, a "family member in the kingdom" of God.[20] These family members are not merely those who had accepted an explicit call to follow Jesus as his disciples, as though he had said: "Whoever among my disciples does the will of God is my brother and sister and mother."

Other statements introduced by "whoever" also did not make Jewishness or discipleship conditions for such a familial relationship with Jesus. He was recalled as settling a dispute about greatness by remarking, "Whoever wants to be first must

---

19. Donahue and Harrington, *The Gospel of Mark*, 292–99, at 294 and 298. See J. P. Meier, *Rethinking the Historical Jesus: A Marginal Jew* (New Haven, CT: Yale University Press, 2009), 4:108–28, 171–81.

20. Hagner, *Matthew 1–13*, 358.

be last of all and servant of all." Then, taking a little child in his arms, he said: "Whoever welcomes one such child in my name welcomes me" (Mark 9:33–37). A startling example of these "whoever" statements comes from a report of Jesus answering an objection to an unnamed exorcist. The man cast out demons in Jesus' name but did not belong to the circle of disciples who followed him. Jesus said, "Do not stop him, for no one who does a deed of power in my name will be able soon afterwards to speak evil of me. Whoever is not against me is for me" (Mark 9:38–39). Anyone who experienced the power of Jesus, even someone who was not publicly one of his disciples, would speak well of him. In making this generalization, Jesus looked beyond the particular case of this "outside" exorcist.

In the case of the little child, Jesus did not specify any Jewishness by saying, "If any Jews welcome any such Jewish child in my name, they welcome me." The "whoever" left matters quite open and could be applied to all human beings who welcome and care for little children. In both the saying about little children and that about the unnamed exorcist, Jesus talked about things done explicitly in his "name"; that condition was absent in the statement about doing the will of God. Here things were left totally open and could be applied to anyone, even to those who had never even heard Jesus' name. This was also the case in the saying about being servant of all. It applied anywhere and to anyone. Jesus challenged assumptions about rank and status that were/are found in many, if not all, cultures. Once again no explicit reference to Jesus was attached, as if he had spoken of being "servant of all" in his name. The teaching applied to people of any place concerned with issues of status in a world that, whether they knew it or not, was being reshaped by the power and presence of God's kingdom.

Beyond question, these "whoever" statements are embedded in the different contexts in which the Gospel writers present Jesus' proclamation of the kingdom to his Jewish audiences. Yet the statements have a generalized form that lifts them above and beyond their specific setting to apply generally to people anywhere.

Third, the *parables* formed a major element when Jesus preached the kingdom.[21] Unquestionably, Jesus addressed them to Jewish audiences. He also gave a few of the parables a Jewish spin (that of the Pharisee and tax collector in Luke 18:10–14) or a Jewish setting in Palestine (that of the Good Samaritan in Luke 10:30–37). Yet characteristically the parables pictured situations repeated in indefinitely many places and times: for instance, a woman searching for a lost coin (Luke 15:8–10) or a woman mixing yeast in the flour she is kneading to bake in the oven (Matt. 13:33). For nearly two thousand years readers around the world have drawn inspiration from the parables. Everywhere and for anyone they can generate insights about God and the reign of God. They have displayed a universal power that takes them far beyond Palestine, the original setting in which Jesus first preached them. They were and are stories told for anyone, not just for insiders.

In his parables Jesus proved himself to be "the" religious storyteller of all time. Much more than mere picturesque illustrations, his parables continue to question readers/hearers anywhere, to challenge their normal standards and securities, and to invite them to walk in radically different ways. His parables revealed a new world and a new way of living for everybody—not merely then and there for his fellow Jews or for those who would make up the church. They did so and continue to do so through language and pictures that seem quite familiar and very ordinary, even if at times Jesus gave his story line unusual and even extraordinary twists.

Jesus tells us of two brothers, the younger one who runs away and the older one who stays at home. He introduces day

---

21. See J. R. Donahue, *The Gospel in Parable: Metaphor, Narrative, and Theology in the Synoptic Gospels* (Philadelphia: Fortress Press, 1981); R. Etchells, *A Reading of the Parables* (London: Darton, Longman & Todd, 1998); A. J. Hultgren, "Parable," in S. E. Balentine (ed.), *The Oxford Encyclopedia of the Bible and Theology* (New York: Oxford University Press, 2015), 2:135–40; G. O'Collins, *Following the Way* (London: HarperCollins, 1999).

laborers who work at harvesting the grapes and managers in charge of large estates. He brings in women searching for lost property or preparing dough for baking. His stories present a lazy judge, a merchant hunting for precious jewels, a traveler robbed and left for dead, a rich man who does nothing for sick and hungry people on the street right outside his house, and servants waiting up at night for their master to return. The parables continue to take people everywhere into the mind and heart of Jesus. The parables let them glimpse his vision of the world around him, a world in which the final reign of God is dawning. These stories fashioned by Jesus answer the universal questions: What is God like? How is God dealing with me? To whom does God show mercy?

When addressing these and similar questions, Jesus significantly did not appeal much to the OT scriptures or to the history of the chosen people. He did appeal to "the God of Abraham, Isaac, and Jacob" but never—at least explicitly—to God as the One who delivered his people from slavery in Egypt. He spoke of God not as the all-powerful king of the exodus and some of the psalms but as the loving Father (*Abba*) who constantly cares for all his creatures (Matt. 6:25–34) and blesses with his rain and sunshine all human beings, even the wicked and unjust (Matt. 5:43–48). In filling out the identity and characteristics of the "Father" with whom the Lord's Prayer begins (Matt. 6:9–13; Luke 11:2–4), Jesus drew on numerous "ordinary" experiences of all people rather than on the specific, Jewish experience of God in their particular history of revelation and salvation.

Fourth, we might cite other areas of Jesus' teaching that illustrate how it was expressed in ways that reached out to everyone: for instance, the beatitudes and the Lord's Prayer.[22] On the one hand, the language (e.g. the "poor" of YHWH and God's name

---

22. For a commentary and rich bibliography on the beatitudes and the Lord's Prayer, see Meier, *A Marginal Jew*, 2:317–36, 377–89 (beatitudes), 291–302, 353–66 (Lord's Prayer). The beatitudes, along with other features of the Sermon on the Mount (Matt. 5–7), helped shape the teaching and practice of Mohandas Gandhi.

being "hallowed") enjoyed a rich OT background, as John Meier shows abundantly. Yet, on the other hand, this language spoke to everyone: for example, "Blessed are the peacemakers" and "Thy will be done." Both here and in the other examples I have quoted above, major themes in the teaching of Jesus touched all human beings and not merely the particular Jewish audience that he addressed. It is plausible to claim that, when he taught, he intended to reach beyond the religious and ethnic frontiers of his specific audience and deliver a message to others as well.

The Love Command

When questioned about "the first commandment," Jesus responded from within the Jewish tradition by *first* quoting the *Shema* ("Hear, O Israel") on the love of God (Deut. 6:4–5) and *then* adding another OT text concerned with the love of one's neighbor (Lev. 19:18). "Hear, O Israel: the Lord our God, the Lord is one; you shall love the Lord your God with all your heart, and with all your soul, and with all your mind, and with all your strength. The second is this. You shall love your neighbor as yourself" (Mark 12:28–34). In the context of the *Shema*, faith in YHWH as "the one and only God" provides the motive for loving God with total love and undivided dedication that holds nothing back—that is, with all one's being ("heart," "soul," "mind," and "strength"). Jesus himself, of course, embodied perfectly the double command of love. He practiced to perfection love for God, whom he called *Abba* ("Father dear"), and love for all human beings. It is much better to sum up his life this way instead of using a negative term to speak of his "utter sinlessness."[23]

In his teaching on love, Jesus innovated in two ways: first, by combining the two classic texts from the Old Testament on love of God and love of neighbor, respectively. He distinguished but would not separate the vertical relationship to God and the

---

23. In *Christology*, 280–84, I wrote of his "sinlessness."

horizontal relationship to one's neighbor. Together they form one commitment of love that transcends all the other commandments in importance, summarizes the key values of the Jewish Torah, and provides a basic framework for understanding and applying the law to God.[24]

The second innovation introduced by Jesus went beyond defining "neighbor" narrowly as one's kin and one's people. In Leviticus 19:18, "neighbor" meant one's fellow Israelites; a few verses later, "neighbor" was slightly extended to "resident aliens" (Lev. 19:33–34; see Job 31:32 on hospitality to strangers). Jesus, however, defined "neighbors" in a way that went beyond family and ethnic relationships and contacts with resident aliens. He spoke even of the need to love one's enemies, whoever they were (Luke 6:27–35 par.).

When Luke records the teaching of Jesus on love for God and neighbor (Luke 10:25–28), he at once has Jesus tell the story of the Good Samaritan in answer to the question, "And who is my neighbor?" (Luke 10:29). Even if this parable may not have originally come from that setting, it certainly comes from Jesus and lets us glimpse his universal application of neighborly love. In this story the hero is neither the Jewish priest nor the Levite but a despised and even hated outsider, a Samaritan. Jesus holds up this compassionate person as an example for everyone, a practical model for all human beings when faced with someone who is distressed and afflicted, and to whom we should "show pity and kindness, even beyond the bounds of one's own ethnic and religious group."[25] The term "Good Samaritan" has entered languages everywhere and become common human patrimony, even for those who have no idea where the expression comes from.

This teaching is also inculcated by a scene that Matthew draws from his special source: the final judgment scene in which "all the nations" and, seemingly, every individual human being

---

24. On the double command of love in the Gospel of Mark, see Meier, *A Marginal Jew*, 4:478–528, 576–613.

25. Fitzmyer, *The Gospel According to Luke X–XXIV*, 884.

will appear before "the Son of Man" (Matt. 25:31–46).[26] He will bring the final blessings of the kingdom in its fullness for the righteous, and will pronounce condemnation for the wicked. The two groups will be, respectively, approved for their deeds of mercy toward Jesus himself ("I was hungry and you gave me food") or faulted for their lack of loving deeds toward him ("I was hungry and you gave me no food"). Jesus lists six common needs (being hungry, thirsty, a stranger, naked, sick, and in prison), which he repeats four times in the text, with a corresponding list of remedies (e.g. "I was a stranger and you welcomed me"). The list is open ended and can be expanded and updated (e.g. "I was ignorant and you taught me," "I was dying and you gave me your blood," and "I was dead and you buried me").

In the perspective of Jesus, those who are in desperate need belong to him; he identifies himself with them; they are members of his family. One's relationship to other people—above all, those in serious need—cannot be divorced from one's relationship to Jesus himself. The scene of final judgment elaborates and universalizes what Jesus says elsewhere about identifying himself with his disciples, with little children, and with others (Matt. 10:40–42; 18:5–6).

The judgment passage leaves us with a question: How could all the people of the world be fairly judged by standards that they may never have heard of? If they had all known Jesus, acknowledged his identity as the incarnate Son of God, and recognized that he took deeds of mercy toward the needy as done to himself, the reward or punishment of every individual at the final judgment would seem justified. But, even if the disciples of Jesus were to proclaim rapidly "the good news of the kingdom" literally "throughout the world" and so bring their "testimony to all the nations" (Matt. 24:14), this missionary outreach would take some time. What of those who die in the meantime without having heard the proclamation? Or those who, with the best will in the world, remain unconvinced by the proclamation? Would the norms of the last judgment be

---

26. See Hagner, *Matthew 14–28*, 737–47; Luz, *Matthew 21–28*, 263–84.

fairly applied to all of them, as the words of Jesus imply? Yes, the standards are universal. All will be judged on the basis of practical love toward the needy.

Here it is worth recalling that the "catalogue of charitable works" converges with "statements from other religions. There is nothing specifically Christian about this list; it appears in similar language in other religions" and—one should add—in the OT and further Jewish sources.[27] In Jesus' picture of the judgment scene, those to be judged (all human beings without exception) did not have to know that they were dealing with Jesus when exercising practical love toward the needy or failing to do so. In this sense the practice of love toward suffering men and women can fairly be the norm of universal judgment.

A further puzzle about the judgment scene arises from what Jesus says to the righteous: "Just as you did it [some work of mercy] to one of these my lowliest brothers, you did it to me" (Matt. 25:40; see 25:45). Some commentators understand "these my brothers" to be needy disciples of Jesus—in particular, itinerant Christian missionaries. After all, elsewhere in Matthew's Gospel, when the family of Jesus arrive to speak with him, Jesus points to his disciples and calls them "my brothers" and "my brother and sister and mother" (Matt. 12:49–50). Nevertheless, what he says in Matthew 25:31–46 occurs in a different context, the final judgment at which "all the nations" will be present. In this context Jesus speaks of his "brothers" (and sisters) as all those who need help, whoever they are and wherever they are—even one's enemies who are in any case to be loved (Matt. 5:43–44). The language of "brothers and sisters" applies far beyond the small group of Jesus' disciples, who in any case are to go on mission to the non-Jews, in fact to "all the nations."

Outside the Cross No Christology of Religions

Thus far, in reflecting on the history of the incarnate Son of God, I have recalled his active relationship with those who did

---

27. Luz, *Matthew 21–28*, 266 n. 30, 269–70, 278 n. 137.

not share his Jewish faith. Jesus reached out to "the others"
through what he did: for a Syro-Phoenician woman, a centurion, a Gerasene demoniac, a deaf-mute, four thousand hungry Gentiles, and a Samaritan leper. In the case of the woman,
the centurion, and the Samaritan leper, Jesus not only did
something for them but he also strongly praised their faith.
Jesus likewise reached across religious frontiers through much
of his preaching of the kingdom of God—a message for everyone rather than a particular call to reform synagogues and/or
to prepare for the institution of the church. As a matter of historical fact, the parable of the Good Samaritan, the beatitudes,
and the double love command (love for God and for neighbor)
have been taken up widely, even by those who have perhaps
never even heard the name of Jesus.

When detailing the relevance of the incarnation for our
Christology of religions, we may not leave matters at that point.
Saint Paul's contrast between Christ crucified and human wisdom (1 Cor. 1:18–2:5) stands in judgment on all theologians
whose reflections on the situation of the "others" stop short
of incorporating Calvary and recognizing God hidden in suffering and in the shame of the crucifixion. Martin Luther's
conviction, *extra crucem nulla theologia* (outside the cross no
theology),[28] censures those many Christian theologians of religion who indulge "human wisdom" by evading the crucified
Christ and refusing to let his crucifixion contribute to what
they have to say about the religious "others."[29]

---

28. Hans-Martin Barth writes: "Luther's whole theology is, we might
say, colored by and soaked in the blood of the Crucified and the suffering of the world," in *The Theology of Luther: A Critical Assessment* (Minneapolis: Fortress Press, 2013), 79.

29. It is sad to recall that none of the hundreds of reviews, articles,
and chapters in books that discussed J. Dupuis, *Toward a Christian
Theology of Religious Pluralism* (Maryknoll, NY: Orbis Books, 1997) noted
the absence of the cross in his theology of religions. Official documents
from the Congregation for the Doctrine of the Faith concerned with
Dupuis also had nothing to say about this absence. For documentation
on this, see D. Kendall and G. O'Collins (eds.), *In Many and Diverse Ways:*

The most mysterious means of divine self-communication, the cross manifests the sinfulness and lostness of *all human beings*. As well as identifying human beings, it identifies God and shows where God continues to be found—in the lives and bodies of those who are crushed and oppressed. The cross reveals that God is not only for us but also with us in our suffering—"us" being understood as all human beings. And yet the cross has failed to attract regular attention from those who specialize in the theology of religions. It has not played the major role in this discipline that it should.[30]

Such neglect appears even stranger when we recall how the execution of Jesus has lodged itself in the memory and imagination of human beings as no other death of an individual ever has. During his lifetime, the appeal of Jesus, if considerable, remained limited to sections of the Palestinian population and proved insufficient to save him from arrest and execution. The wider world knew nothing of him and did not draw its breath in horror and mourn his passing, as it did many centuries later when Mohandas Gandhi and Martin Luther King Jr. were assassinated. But the "postmortem" appeal of the crucified (and risen) Jesus has spread throughout the entire world. Christian believers claim that by his death (and resurrection) he liberated humankind from the power of evil and reconciled it with God (2 Cor. 5:19). Among the millions of "others" who do not accept that claim or have never even heard of it, very many, however, know at least

---

In Honor of Jacques Dupuis (Maryknoll, NY: Orbis Books, 2003), 270–81. It is only in the last couple of years that I have come to recognize the relevance of the cross for any theology (better Christology) of religions. On the widespread neglect of the cross in contemporary theology, see Fleming Rutledge, *The Crucifixion: Understanding the Death of Jesus Christ* (Grand Rapids, MI: Eerdmans, 2015).

30. The deepest human response to the mystery of suffering and evil is found in art: poetry (e.g. the tragedies of Shakespeare), powerful narratives (e.g. the great Russian novels), the visual arts (e.g. the Rondanini Pietà of Michelangelo and the paintings of Francis Bacon), and music (e.g. the Leningrad Symphony of Shostakovich).

vaguely the historical background of the sign of the cross and something of what it can symbolize.[31]

Through his picture of the last judgment (Matt. 25:31–46) Jesus showed how he identified himself in a special way with all human beings who suffer by being abandoned, victimized, and even murdered in the millions. His solidarity with suffering humanity proved a prelude to Calvary, where he would die as a condemned criminal by public execution. Unlike the birds with their nests and the foxes with their lairs, Jesus had "nowhere to lay his head" (Matt. 8:20). He became a homeless person, who sometimes "slept rough." He experienced conflicts when groups and individuals quickly emerged to oppose and even menace him. Seemingly early in his ministry, he had turned into "a man on the run," at times slipping away from murderous-minded enemies who gathered with stunning speed and made attempts on his life (Mark 3:6; Luke 4:28–30; 13:32–35; John 8:59).

At the end he was betrayed by Judas, abandoned by the male disciples, and condemned to death by kangaroo courts presided over by religious authorities and military leaders. In thousands of ways human beings have proved themselves prone to seek out and destroy one another. Jesus died by a particularly horrible form of torture killing. Execution by crucifixion was a hideous combination of impalement and display that was practiced by the masters of the Mediterranean world and involved a leisurely, horrifyingly painful way of dying.

An agricultural image used in John's Gospel can blank out the obscene sadism and unspeakable pain of crucifixion: "unless a grain of wheat falls into the earth and dies, it remains alone; but if it dies, it bears much fruit" (John 12:24). The soft sense of Mother Earth beguiles us. It is with slow gentleness

---

31. On the crucifixion, see R. E. Brown, *The Death of the Messiah*, 2 vols. (New York: Doubleday, 1994); M. Hengel, *The Cross and the Son of God* (London: SCM Press, 1986), 93–185; J. Marcus, *Mark 9–16* (New Haven, CT: Yale University Press, 2009), 924–1078; G. O'Collins, "Crucifixion," *ABD*, 1:1207–10.

and not with awful and abrupt pain that the plant grows from the seed. Human lust for evil struck Jesus down. He fell into the hands of murderous men. He did not slip quietly into the arms of Sister Death.

A principle such as "From death comes life" plays down both the agony and the evil of Calvary. We should insist: "From murder came life," or "In crucifixion God gave life." That was the startling way in which God worked. The exodus from Egypt had been strange enough. God formed his special nation out of a group of runaway slaves. But through the crucifixion he created the world's redeemer out of a murdered man, and his new people out of those who wished to identify with this violent death. "Do you not know," Paul wrote, "that all of us who have been baptized into Christ Jesus were baptized into his death? We were buried with him by baptism into death" (Rom. 6:3–4).

Calvary echoes through what the risen Christ has to say about the apostolic suffering of Paul: "My grace is sufficient for you, for my power is made perfect in weakness" (2 Cor. 12:9). This short sentence, the only words of the risen Lord in Paul's letters, turns us toward the crucifixion. We might imagine the risen Christ looking back and saying about himself: "When I was weak, then I was strong" (2 Cor. 12:10). But what logic controls the coincidence of power and weakness? None, I suspect, that we can fashion. We simply have to allow that the God who acts in surprising ways outdid himself in making a sordid killing the place where he effectively began to inaugurate the final kingdom. On Calvary the loser was the champion, the victim became the hero. He hung there "as poor, yet making many rich, as having nothing, and yet possessing everything" (2 Cor. 6:10).

The body of Christ on the cross disclosed for all time how the Son of God drew near to human beings in their suffering. He is mysteriously but truly present to those who suffer anywhere and at any time and, in particular, to those thousands of innocent victims who every month and even every week suffer violent death. His death on Calvary between two criminals, who presumably had not been followers of Jesus, symbolizes forever his close solidarity with all men and women who are victimized by others—a love that made him vulnerable to the end.

As we have seen, this identification with human pain was also revealed by the criteria for the final judgment (Matt. 25:31–46). The final blessing of the kingdom will come to those who, even without recognizing Christ, meet his needs in the people who suffer by being hungry, thirsty, strangers, naked, sick, or imprisoned. Blaise Pascal's reflection ("He will be in agony to the end of the world") has classically articulated the crucified Christ's enduring presence in the mystery of all human suffering,[32] whether those who suffer are Christ's followers, adherents of "other" religious faiths, or of no such faith at all. To express the worldwide presence of Christ in all who suffer, we could well say: "Where there is suffering there is Christ (ubi dolor, ibi Christus)." It is Christ who is constantly revealed on the cross of human suffering: "Where there is the cross, there is Christ (ubi crux, ibi Christus)."

Any theology of the religions that is truly Christian should incorporate the cross. At the end of his earthly life, the incarnate Son of God showed his worldwide solidarity with all human beings who suffer. Sadly, theologies of religion have regularly ignored the horror of Calvary and what it signifies.

The Relationship to Others Transformed

This chapter has examined how the historical Jesus related to "outsiders" through what he did, taught, and, finally, suffered. Death, burial, resurrection, ascension into glory, and the outpouring of the Holy Spirit at Pentecost transformed that relationship. A final saying from the earthly Jesus about the kingdom of God (Mark 14:25) helps bring this transformation into focus.

---

32. Listed as *Pensée* 552 in such editions of Pascal's *Pensées* as W. F. Trotter's translation (New York: E. P. Dutton, 1958), which follows the standard Brunschvicg edition, this *Pensée* is numbered 919 in A. J. Krailsheimer's translation (Harmondsworth: Penguin, 1966), which adopts the order of the *Pensées* as Pascal left them at his death in 1662.

From the start of his ministry Jesus had announced the divine rule to be at hand.[33] Jesus saw suffering and persecution as characterizing the coming of that kingdom. The message of the kingdom led more or less straight to the mystery of the passion. That message involved a suffering ordeal to come: a time of crisis and distress that was to move toward the day of the Son of Man (Mark 13 parr.), the restoration of Israel (Matt. 19:28 par.), the banquet of the saved, and the salvation of the nations (Matt. 8:11 par.). Thus the arrest, trial, and crucifixion of Jesus dramatized the very thing that totally engaged him— the rule of God that was to come through a time of ordeal.

At the Last Supper Jesus linked his imminent death with the divine kingdom: "Amen, I say to you, I shall not drink again of the fruit of the vine until I drink it new in the kingdom of God" (Mark 14:25 par.).[34] It is widely agreed that this verse has not been shaped by the Eucharistic liturgy of the early church. It derives from what Jesus said during his last meal with his friends. His death is approaching; he will not have another occasion to enjoy a festive meal of any kind. But after his death God will vindicate Jesus and his cause by fully establishing the divine kingdom. Jesus will be seated at the final banquet—obviously with others at his side—when he "drinks wine anew." He looks forward with hope to that final time of eschatological feasting.

In this saying the death of Jesus is implicit, since what we call "the Last Supper" will be the last festive meal of his life. The resurrection as such is not mentioned, but God, it is implied, will rescue Jesus out of death and let him enjoy the final banquet. The saying as such does not attribute to Jesus any redemptive function in the final triumph of the kingdom. It is not stated, or at least not explicitly stated, that he will restore the fellowship with his disciples that will be broken by his arrest and

---

33. On Jesus' proclamation of the kingdom, see Meier, *A Marginal Jew*, 2:289–506.

34. On this verse see ibid., 302–9, 366–71; and Marcus, *Mark 9–16*, 958–59, 967–68.

death—let alone that he will mediate to others their access to the final banquet.

Taken by itself, Mark 14:25 leaves much unsaid. Yet it turns up in Mark's Gospel as *the final kingdom saying* from Jesus, a saying about the kingdom that is connected with his imminent death. The saying is illuminated by all that Jesus has already said. He has constantly preached the future reign of God, which will be *the* saving event for all human beings. By linking his approaching death with the coming kingdom, Jesus implicitly interprets his death as somehow salvific for all. Through his preaching he has promised salvation for human beings at large. Now he associates his death with communion at the final banquet in the coming kingdom of God. The kingdom saying at the Last Supper may be laconic. But it is charged with meaning through all that Jesus has already said about the future kingdom.

It is hardly surprising that Jesus made such a positive integration between the coming kingdom and his own death. The message about the divine reign was inseparable from the person of Jesus. This essential connection between the message of Jesus and his person meant that the vindication of his person in and beyond death involved the vindication of God's kingdom, and vice versa—a vindication that entailed salvation for all humanity.

Here one could press on and introduce a detailed examination of what Jesus said and did at the Last Supper when instituting the new covenant. Such an examination would support the conclusion that he understood his violent death as somehow redemptive for Jew and Gentile alike. Faced with death, Jesus interpreted it as a redemptive service for all human beings, which was to bring a new covenant between God and humanity.[35]

---

35. See G. O'Collins, "Dying and Rising for All?" in G. O'Collins, *Salvation for All: God's Other Peoples* (Oxford: Oxford University Press, 2008), 100–20; S. Hahn and J. Bergsma, "Covenant," in S. E. Balentine

We turn now to the post-Easter situation and the risen Christ's high-priestly intercession for all people: for Buddhists, Christians, Confucians, Hindus, Muslims, Sikhs, followers of traditional religions and the rest—not forgetting agnostics, atheists, and all those millions of people who follow no religious faith at all. The ongoing priesthood of Christ, like his cross, belongs squarely to a Christology of religions. But this priesthood has suffered an astonishing neglect.

(ed.), *The Oxford Encyclopedia of Bible and Theology* (New York: Oxford University Press, 2015), 1:151–66.

2

Christ's High-Priestly Intercession for All

With Christ's resurrection from the dead and ascension to heavenly glory, along with the sending of the Holy Spirit and the birth of the Christian church at Pentecost, the mission of the Son of God and the mission of the Spirit entered a final stage that would be consummated at the end of world history. During his earthly ministry for the kingdom of God, (a) many men and women had spontaneously attached themselves to Jesus: for instance, Bartimaeus who followed him from Jericho to Jerusalem (Mark 10:52); and Mary Magdalene and many other women who had followed Jesus in Galilee and then witnessed his crucifixion in Jerusalem (Mark 15:40–41). At some point during that ministry, Jesus chose from the wider group of his disciples (b) Peter and eleven other men to be special leaders in his movement (Mark 3:13–19 parr.). But neither group (a) nor group (b) underwent any formal rite of passage such as baptism or a form of "ministerial ordination." Along with group (a) and group (b), the earthly Jesus, as we saw in the opening chapter, exercised some ministry toward group (c), Gentile outsiders. As far as we know, those who belonged to group (c) did not enter the ranks of his disciples but simply crossed his path (e.g. the Syro-Phoenician woman and an anonymous deaf mute in Mark 7:24–37). With the Last Supper, the crucifixion, the resurrection, the ascension, and Pentecost, the existence and activity of Jesus himself were radically transformed (1 Cor. 15:35–58), and so too was his relationship to the three groups.

In the case of group (a), faith in the crucified and risen Jesus now involved a formal entrance into the church through a once-and-for-all baptism, the gift of the Holy Spirit, and initiation into a fellowship that involved celebrating the Eucharist "in memory" of Jesus (Acts 2:17–42; Rom. 6:3–11; 1 Cor. 6:11; 11:23–34). As regards (b), leadership by the Twelve grew and changed, with Paul (and others) being called to become an "apostle" and such ministries as "overseers," "presbyters," and "deacons" emerging.[1]

The coming of the church, with its various communities being founded around the Mediterranean and beyond, did not replace the wider reality preached by Jesus—the kingdom of God breaking into the world. Unquestionably, the kingdom and the church should not be separated, whether we deal with the first century (and the developments from Jesus to Paul) or with the world today. But we forget at our peril that the church is there to serve the kingdom and not vice versa. The distinction remains essential for understanding the situation of those who have not (or have not yet) embraced Christian faith and baptism.

After the resurrection and exaltation of Jesus, the apostles and other early Christians "went out and proclaimed the good news everywhere, while *the Lord worked with them and confirmed the message by the signs that accompanied it*" (Mark 16:20). The author of this additional ending to Mark witnessed here to the belief and experience of early Christians that the exalted Christ remained dynamically present in their mission to preach, baptize, and celebrate the Eucharist. Eventually this belief flowered in St. Augustine's teaching on the invisible Christ (and not the visible minister, being the primary minister of baptism[2]) and in convictions about Christ's priestly presence in the celebration

---

1. On the founding of the church and its emerging leaders, see G. O'Collins, *Rethinking Fundamental Theology* (Oxford: Oxford University Press, 2011), 265–91.

2. See G. O'Collins and M. K. Jones, *Jesus Our Priest: A Christian Approach to Christ's Priesthood* (Oxford: Oxford University Press, 2010), 95–96.

of the Eucharist (and, indeed, of all the other sacraments). He
continued to be present and "work with" the church in its liturgical and sacramental life.

But what of Christ's relationship to the "outsiders," those
millions who have succeeded the "Gentiles" to whom Jesus
occasionally ministered during the final years of his earthly
life? This relationship has featured extensively in what numerous Roman Catholics and other Christians have written on the
theology of religions. But in all that literature, as far as I can
see, no one has set out to reflect on other faiths in the light
of the priesthood of Jesus Christ. Without alleging that his
priesthood should be seen as the only approach to be adopted
in this field, nevertheless, I believe, as will be argued below,
that the theme of his priesthood pulls together much of what
Christian thinkers would, or at least should, want to deal with
when reflecting on other living faiths. But so far the light that
Christ's priesthood throws on those of other faiths and, in general, his priestly relationship to "outsiders" remain an untold
story. What one might call this "sacerdotal existential" should
be explored.

The failure of those who have developed a theology of religions to appeal to the intercessory power of Christ the high
priest belongs to a widespread neglect of his priesthood as
such, which has gone on for centuries. When writing, with
Michael Keenan Jones, *Jesus Our Priest: A Christian Approach to
the Priesthood of Christ*,[3] I discovered how very few theologians
have ever examined the priesthood of Christ. If theologians
remain prone to neglect the priesthood of Christ, it would be
strange to find them introducing into the theology of religion
themes about the priestly intercession of Christ. But why have
so many theologians neglected the priesthood of Christ and
its intercessory power? That was a question Jones and I repeatedly grappled with in the five chapters (Chaps. 5–9) that made
up the heart of our joint work. For possible answers, I refer
readers to those chapters.

---

3. See ibid.

Karl Rahner, Jacques Dupuis, T. F. Torrance, and Robert J. Sherman

Before exploring what the priesthood of Christ contributes to a theology of religions, let me illustrate the general neglect of this theme by first sampling the work of two leading authors in this area: Karl Rahner (1904–84) and Jacques Dupuis (1923–2004). Both shaped what many Christians have thought about the followers of other religions (and those who do not practice any religious faith at all). Rahner, along with various theologians in Asia, Europe, and elsewhere, prepared the way for the relevant teaching of the Second Vatican Council (1962–65) that is found, especially but not solely, in the Dogmatic Constitution on the Church (*Lumen Gentium,* of November 21, 1964) and the Declaration on the Relation of the Church to Non-Christian Religions (*Nostra Aetate,* of October 28, 1965). But neither Rahner nor Dupuis introduced Christ's priesthood into their theology of religions.

Starting from a lecture he delivered in April 1961, "Christianity and the Non-Christian Religions,"[4] Rahner often returned to this and closely related themes in essays included in *Theological Investigations*[5] and in *Foundations of Christian Faith*.[6] Yet he never reflected on other religions and their followers in the light of Christ's priesthood. It would have been surprising if he had done so, since in all his writing he had little to say theologically about that priesthood.

What Rahner wrote about Christ's priesthood turned up in spiritual reflections offered to those about to be ordained to the priestly ministry or already exercising that ministry.

---

4. K. Rahner, "Christianity and the Non-Christian Religions," *Theological Investigations* (London: Darton, Longman & Todd, 1966), 5:115–34.

5. In the twenty-three volumes of Rahner's *Theological Investigations* (London: Darton, Longman & Todd, 1961–92), the theme of Christ/Christianity and "the others" recurred frequently and was treated at chapter length in vols. 5, 6, 9, 12, 14, 16, 17, and 18.

6. K. Rahner, *Foundations of Christian Faith: An Introduction to the Idea of Christianity* (New York: Seabury Press, 1978), 126–33, 138–75.

Both in Germany and in Rome, Rahner gave eight-day courses of prayers, based on the *Spiritual Exercises* of St. Ignatius, to young, German-speaking candidates for the priesthood. Many of these meditations were edited and printed in 1965, and in the same year were translated and published in English.[7] Rahner closed the section of the retreat that corresponded to the "second week" of the *Exercises* with a meditation on the priesthood. The opening page dealt briefly with the priesthood of Christ, about which Rahner made two points. First, from the moment that the Word takes on a human existence, he is "essentially God's high priest."[8] Here Rahner followed St. John Chrysostom and many others in the Christian tradition when firmly stating that the priesthood of Christ and its exercise began with the incarnation.[9] Second, Rahner understood that Christ as priest "pours out God's love" on "the whole world," and "makes possible the holy conversation" between "God and the whole world."[10] Linking "the whole world" with the exercise of Christ's priesthood might, in another context, have led Rahner to reflect on the followers of other religions and the followers of none. But, given the audience for whom he was developing the meditation, he moved at once to speak of "our priesthood," "our priestly existence," and "our priestly life."[11]

In a 1967 book, published the following year in English,[12] Rahner wrote of the greatness and the burden of the priesthood. Addressed chiefly to his fellow priests, the chapters originated in ordination sermons, jubilee sermons, retreat conferences, essays, lectures, and prayers. Once again he did not focus on the priesthood of Christ himself. The book includes a chapter on "Christ the Exemplar of Priestly Obedience" and a "Prayer for the Right Spirit of Christ's Priesthood" (which

---

7. K. Rahner, *Spiritual Exercises* (New York: Herder & Herder, 1965).
8. Ibid., 203–4.
9. O'Collins and Jones, *Jesus Our Priest*, 80, 241–43.
10. Rahner, *Spiritual Exercises*, 204.
11. Ibid., 204–9.
12. K. Rahner, *Servants of the Lord* (London: Burns & Oates, 1968).

began by calling Christ "high priest of all human beings").[13] Yet in both the chapter and the prayer, Rahner directed his attention to those exercising ordained ministry in the church and did not set himself to explore the priesthood of Christ himself, let alone connect that priesthood with the "all human beings" and the religions of the world. In some related publications listed at the end of the book, we find that Rahner maintained steadily the same primary focus: on the life and ministry of ordained priests rather than on Christ's own priesthood.[14]

Finally, Rahner retrieved some conferences that he had given in 1961 to candidates for priestly ordination and published them in 1970.[15] The conferences were intended to encourage his hearers to understand more deeply and accept more devoutly a priestly way of life. For Rahner, ordained priesthood embodied selfless, loving service of others and of God's coming kingdom. Yet again the focus of the book allowed only for incidental references to Christ's own priesthood and certainly not for any lines being drawn between that priesthood and world religions. Even when Rahner spoke of the "continuation of Christ's priesthood," he was primarily concerned to show how Catholic priests unite a prophetical calling with a cultic role.[16]

To sum up: from the end of the 1960s and right through the 1970s, Rahner wrote about the priestly office and the spirituality of priests. But he developed his reflections without first establishing any detailed theology of Christ's high priesthood, from which he could then draw some conclusions about the work and spiritual life of those who share in that priesthood through ordination.[17]

---

13. Ibid., 127–48, 213–16.

14. Ibid., 217–18.

15. K. Rahner, *Meditations on Priestly Life* (London: Sheed & Ward, 1973).

16. Ibid., 103–6.

17. K. Rahner, "The Point of Departure in Theology for Determining the Nature of the Priestly Office," and "Theological Reflections on the Priestly Image of Today and Tomorrow," *Theological Investiga-*

Jacques Dupuis, at greater length than Rahner, constructed over many years a theology of religions. This work climaxed with *Toward a Christian Theology of Religious Pluralism* and *Christianity and the Religions*.[18] In both books he discussed the "mediation" exercised by Christ,[19] but he did not characterize that mediation as "priestly." It was only once in either of the books that he ever spoke about Christ as "priest" or "high priest," and that was in a passage where he was concerned with Melchizedek, "the type of him who will be the eternal High Priest."[20]

From his first publication in 1960 right through to 2003, Dupuis often wrote about various Christological questions, and in 1994 he published a major work, *Who Do You Say I Am? Introduction to Christology*.[21] But in no book or article did he ever explore the nature of Christ's priesthood. Hence, the high priesthood of Christ was not evidenced in either his theology of religions or his reflections in Christology. At best, like Rahner, he only touched on Christ's priesthood, and that was when reviewing four books on ordained priesthood (in 1971, 1975, and 1978) and publishing four brief articles on the same topic (two in 1975, and one in both 1975 and 1979).[22]

tions (London: Darton, Longman & Todd, 1974), 12:31–38, 39–60; K. Rahner, "The Spirituality of the Secular Priest," and "The Spirituality of the Priest in the Light of His Office," *Theological Investigations* (1983), 19:103–16, 117–38.

18. J. Dupuis, *Toward a Christian Theology of Religious Pluralism* (Maryknoll, NY: Orbis Books, 1997); J. Dupuis, *Christianity and the Religions: From Confrontation to Dialogue* (Maryknoll, NY: Orbis Books, 2002).

19. Dupuis, *Toward a Christian Theology*, 186, 307; this latter passage is repeated almost word for word in *Christianity and the Religions*, 168–69.

20. Dupuis, *Toward a Christian Theology*, 37.

21. J. Dupuis, *Who Do You Say I Am? Introduction to Christology* (Maryknoll, NY: Orbis Books, 1994); in this book Dupuis never mentions the Christological title of "priest." For a complete bibliography of Dupuis's publications, see Daniel Kendall and Gerald O'Collins (eds.), *In Many and Diverse Ways: In Honor of Jacques Dupuis* (Maryknoll, NY: Orbis Books, 2003), 231–69.

22. For details, see Kendall and O'Collins, *In Many and Diverse*

Rahner, Dupuis, and other specialists in the theology of religions, as I found, failed to explore possibilities offered by Christ's priesthood being exercised for the benefit of all humankind. Perhaps, I fondly imagined, theologians who write on that priesthood—or at least a few of them—might apply some of their conclusions to the situation of those who follow "other" faiths or follow none at all. Then I discovered to my astonishment how few theologians, both in the past and in modern times, have investigated the priesthood of Christ.[23]

One of those very few to do so was T. F. Torrance (1913–2007).[24] When elucidating the identity and work of Christ as priest, he engaged fully with the Gospel accounts of the Last Supper, with the Letter to the Hebrews, and with the Eucharist in the life of the church. Through Jesus' "self-consecration" and "high-priestly intercession" at the Last Supper, Torrance explained, he intended that his disciples should be "presented to the Father through his own self-offering on their behalf." Synthesizing the witness of Hebrews and the Gospels and respecting the mission of the Holy Spirit allowed Torrance to understand the Eucharist as the priestly presence of the self-offering of the incarnate, crucified, risen, and ascended Christ—a sacrificial self-offering in which the faithful share.[25]

The Eucharist, for Torrance, "is Christ himself who is really present pouring out his Spirit upon us, drawing us into the power of his vicarious life, death and resurrection, and uniting us with his self-oblation and self-presentation before the face of the Father where he ever lives to make intercession for us." Thus the Eucharist is "what it is" because of its "grounding" in "what God in Christ has done, does do, and will do for us in

---

Ways, 236, 239, and 242 (for the reviews), and 235, 238 and 243 (for the articles).

23. For details of this perennial neglect of Christ's priesthood, see O'Collins and Jones, *Jesus Our Priest,* passim; our bibliography (294–96) shows how very few have written on that priesthood in modern times.

24. T. F. Torrance, *Theology in Reconciliation: Essays Toward Evangelical and Catholic Unity in East and West* (Eugene, OR: Wipf & Stock, 1996).

25. Ibid., 107, 108, 110.

his Spirit." In the celebration of the Eucharist Christ acts by assimilating us in mind and will to himself and lifting us up to the closest union with himself in the identity of himself as Offerer and Offering to the presence of the Father.[26]

While making a notable contribution to a Christian understanding of Christ's priesthood, Torrance did not examine what this priesthood means for the wider world. He reflected on the relationship between Christ's priesthood and his disciples, "we" who are united with his self-offering and lifted into the closest, priestly union with him.

Another, more recent, writer, Robert J. Sherman also writes admirably of Christ's "priestly mediation and intercession," which "make Christian worship possible in the first place. Christ is *our heavenly high priest, the head of the Church,* enabling all who minister or worship in his name."[27] But does Christ exercise his priesthood only for members of the church who assemble for Christian worship? Do the baptized monopolize the attention of Christ as "our heavenly high priest," so that he is not high priest for all the other human beings, many of whom may never have heard his name? Without argument, Sherman seems to have instinctively limited the beneficiaries of Christ's priestly office to the members of the church.

After examining Rahner, Dupuis, Torrance, Sherman, and other modern theologians, I came to two negative conclusions. First, those (many) who write on other living faiths do not introduce the priesthood of Christ into their discussion. Second, those (very few) who write on Christ's priesthood have not appreciated the possibilities it offers for a theology of religions or, better, a Christology of religions. What story would I now propose about the high priesthood of Christ and the light it sheds on the revealing and saving self-communication of God to those of other faiths?

---

26. Ibid., 107, 118.
27. R. J. Sherman, "Christ the Priest: The Son's Sacrificial Offering," *King, Priest, and Prophet: A Trinitarian Theology of Atonement* (New York/London: T. & T. Clark, 2004), 169–218, at 218; italics mine.

Hebrews

The Letter to the Hebrews stands apart by containing the only explicit biblical narrative of Christ as priest and by portraying him extensively in the exercise of his high priesthood. The vision of Christ as eternal high priest makes its first appearance in Hebrews and seems a self-consciously avant-garde interpretation of Christ's life, death, and exaltation. Written between 60 and 95 CE (more plausibly before 70) and sent to Italy (Rome?) from Ephesus (Heb. 13:23–24), Hebrews is an anonymous sermon aimed at encouraging members of a particular community, which had earlier suffered considerable hardships (10:32–34), to maintain their faith and hope. They may be facing further persecutions (13:3). Some of them could be already "slipping away" (2:1), in danger of letting their hearts become "hardened by sin" (3:13), being threatened by "strange teaching" (13:9), and even abandoning their faith in Christ (3:12; 6:4–6; 12:25). Certain individuals are already staying away from the liturgical meetings of the community (10:25).[28]

All these particular circumstances leave us with the question: does Hebrews, while expounding the priesthood of Christ, envisage its impact affecting only a specific Christian community or, perhaps, other such communities suffering from similar challenges? From some particular "scraps," can we create a compelling narrative of Christ as high priest who exercises a universal office and offers salvation to the whole world?

Priesthood and sacrifice are correlative terms—something taken for granted by the author of Hebrews (8:3). The priestly practices outlined in sections of the Pentateuch that he recalls

---

28. On Hebrews, see Harold Attridge, *The Epistle to the Hebrews* (Philadelphia: Fortress Press, 1989); Craig R. Koester, *Hebrews* (New York: Doubleday, 2001); and Peter T. O'Brien, *The Letter to the Hebrews* (Grand Rapids, MI: Eerdmans, 2010); for Hebrews on priesthood, see John M. Scholer, *Proleptic Priests: Priesthood in the Epistle to the Hebrews* (Sheffield: Sheffield Academic Press, 1991).

involved offering sacrifices of animals. When he mentions for the first time the *priestly* identity of Christ, he links it at once to Christ's *sacrificial* activity: he became "a merciful and faithful high priest to expiate the sins of the people" (2:17). In the context, "people" points, at least immediately, to the descendants of Abraham and Sarah and not to the human race in general. Nevertheless, the author of Hebrews envisages a group that is much broader than the one he addresses, a particular community that is being "tested" (2:18).

The horizon that the letter proceeds to open up will be as large as the whole human race. The author lists three qualifications that made Jesus the high priest of the new dispensation: "every high priest is [1] taken from among human beings (*anthrōpōn*) and [2] appointed on behalf of human beings (*anthrōpōn*) with respect to the matters pertaining to God, [3] in order to offer gifts and sacrifices for sin" (5:1). In other words, as high priest, Christ has been (1) chosen from among human beings, and (2) not self-appointed, but called by God to represent them (3) in the sacrificial offering he makes, in particular for the expiation of their sins.

Through taking on the human condition in the incarnation (1:1–4), the Son of God satisfied the first condition. As high priest he could represent (all) human beings, precisely because he shared their condition, including growth, suffering, and death (5:5–9). The opening verses of Hebrews 5 address explicitly the (three) requirements that qualified Christ for his role as high priest. Elsewhere Hebrews fills out the (first) priestly requirement of "being taken from among human beings." As "high priest" he could "sympathize" with "our weaknesses" by being tested/tempted in all ways (4:15). In "the days of his flesh" he prayed, and did so in painful and threatening situations (5:7). He grew, was tested, and made perfect through suffering (2:10, 18), above all through enduring death (2:9, 14; 5:7), a death by crucifixion (6:6).

Jesus shared and shares humanity with all human beings, who are "the children" of the one God and Father, "for whom and through whom all things exist" (2:10). As "originator" of their salvation, Christ goes before his "brothers and sisters" to deliver them from being enslaved to the fear and power of death (2:10–15). This passage will specify these "brothers and sisters" as "the descendants of Abraham" (2:16). Nevertheless, it is "sharing" the same human "flesh and blood" (2:14) through being created by the one divine Father that makes the one human family, who have been delivered by the high priestly work of Christ. He became high priest not only for the descendants of Abraham but also for all who belong to the human family.

While death and exaltation proved the defining moment of Christ's priesthood, a priestly self-offering characterized his whole human existence (10:5–7). From the start, Hebrews links his priestly activity of purifying sin (1:2–4) with the incarnation, through which he entered into solidarity with all human beings. The incarnation allowed the Son of God to become a high priest for everyone.

This global perspective also builds on the priest-king Melchizedek, who blesses Abraham (Gen. 14:17–20) and is called a "priest forever" (Ps. 110:4). The mysterious person of Melchizedek provides a figure who is both prior to and superior to the (Jewish) Levitical priests. After three times attributing to Christ an eternal priesthood "according to the order of Melchizedek" (5:6, 10; 6:20), the author of Hebrews comes clean, so to speak, with his strategy: the priesthood of the mysterious priest-king was earlier and greater than the Levitical priesthood (7:1–28). Since the scriptures do not mention Melchizedek's ancestors, birth, or death, he "remains" a priest forever (7:3), unlike the Levitical priests who all died and could not continue in office forever. Abraham gave Melchizedek a tenth of the spoils from a victory over "the kings" and received a blessing from him, thus showing how Melchizedek was greater than Abraham and his descendant Levi (the head of the priestly tribe). With the cornerstone of Melchizedek in place, Hebrews presses on to argue that, being a "priest forever according to the order of Melchizedek," Christ is superior to any Levitical high priest. He "holds his priesthood permanently" and "always lives to make intercession" for those who "approach God through him" (7:24–25). Thus, Christ is not only a priest for everyone (see above) but for always. His priesthood is exercised for all people and for all time (and beyond).

As high priest, Christ functions as the "mediator of a new covenant" (9:15; 12:24). The new covenant provides a linchpin, without which Hebrews would fall apart. This definitive commitment of God is interpreted against the background of the Mosaic covenant with the Jewish people but stands in contrast with it as the "better" or fully efficacious covenant (8:7–13). But does this covenant brought about by Christ the high priest apply to the whole human race? At first glance, it appears to be limited to Christian believers.

Christ's sacrifice, Hebrews declares, has opened a new and living way into the presence of God and allows his followers to move in hope toward the inner shrine of heaven, where Jesus their "forerunner" and high priest belongs forever (10:19–20). They can continue to appropriate Christ's self-offering, knowing that he constantly "appears in the presence of God" on their behalf (9:24; see 6:20). Christ's priestly journey into the heavenly sanctuary has ended with his sitting at the right hand of God (1:3). But for his followers his priesthood continues forever, inasmuch as he "lives always" to "make intercession" for those who "approach God through him" (7:25). But what of all "the others"?

Sometimes Hebrews seems comprehensive in its proposals about the beneficiaries of Christ's priestly work. Jesus, it announces, "tasted [experienced] death for everyone" (2:9). Yet it can also propose that he "became the source of eternal salvation [only?] for all who obey him" (5:9). Receiving the offer of salvation prompts believers into following Jesus on the journey of faith. What then of those who, through no fault of their own, have never heard of Jesus and thus are not in a position to repent of their sins, "obey" him, be delivered from death, and enjoy in glory the presence of God? It seems that for Hebrews salvation is available only to those who know of Christ's priestly work, approach God's "throne of grace" to "receive mercy" for past sins, and find grace for present and future "need" (4:10). Is the possibility of salvation through the new covenant restricted to those who consciously approach the royal throne of God through Jesus the high priest (7:25)?

A roll call of heroes and heroines of faith (11:1–12:1) does not list any Christians but only those who lived before Christ and hence could not consciously have accepted redemption coming through his priestly work. Not surprisingly, Hebrews proposes in chapter 11 an "open" version of faith: "the reality of things hoped for" and "the proof of things not seen. By this [faith] the elders [our ancestors] received approval. By faith we understand that the universe was fashioned by the Word of God, so that from what cannot be seen that which is seen has come into being" (11:1–3). A further verse adds two (rather general) requirements to this "open" account of faith: "without faith it is impossible to please God; for whoever would approach him must believe that he exists and that he rewards those who seek him" (11:6).

The opening three verses of Hebrews 11 highlight faith but say little about its content. The passage hints at the future. Divine promises (presumably of some eternal inheritance) have aroused the hope of human beings and their trust that God will keep these promises, which concern future things that are "not seen." Faith also involves a conviction about the past. One understands by faith the unseen origin of the world: it was "fashioned by the Word of God." Just as people of faith rely on the Word of God about the *genesis* of the universe, so too do they rely on the Word of God's promise when considering the *goal* of the world and of their own existence. Both in their view of the past and their hope for the future, the lives of those who have faith are intertwined with the life of the invisible God.

This account of faith makes no mention of Christ. He will appear later, when the list of heroes and heroines of faith reaches the figure of Jesus, "the pioneer and perfector of faith" (12:2). The opening verses of Hebrews 11 have invoked "the elders" or "ancestors," people whom God honored for their persevering faith. Then follow examples of those who have lived on the basis of faith, with particular attention paid to Abraham, Sarah, and Moses. Some of those who exemplify faith (Abel, Enoch, and Noah) existed prior to Abraham, Sarah, and the formation of the chosen people. One figure of faith is "Rahab the prostitute," an outsider who belonged to the story of the conquest of the promised land (Josh. 2:1–24; 6:22–25).

Hebrews 11:6 lets us glimpse the shape that the faith of outsiders can take. "Pleasing God" means doing the divine will, in particular, through deeds of kindness and service of others (13:16, 20–21). Such conduct need not depend on a conscious relationship with Christ the high priest. A faith that "pleases" God is a possibility open to all. Likewise, "approaching" God in prayer does not necessarily depend on an awareness of the priestly intercession of the exalted Christ. That intercession functions, whether or not worshipers are conscious of the priestly presence of Christ when they draw near to God in prayer. These and further aspects of Hebrews 11:6 spell out an "open" account of faith. Salvation through such faith is offered to all people and offered on the basis of the self-sacrificing priesthood of Christ, even if they are not (or are not yet) in a position to follow him in conscious obedience on the pilgrimage of faith.[29] We return in a later chapter to the possibilities of faith for "others" offered by Hebrews.

When pursuing the biblical witness to the relationship between the priestly work of Christ and the salvation offered to all people, Hebrews is the standout. It is the one NT book that gives him the title of "priest" (six times) or "high priest" (ten times). Nevertheless, strands of teaching from other NT authors also illuminate the priesthood of Christ and not least its impact on the whole human race.[30] Let me limit myself to Paul and John.

---

29. See further G. O'Collins, *Salvation for All: God's Other Peoples* (Oxford: Oxford University Press, 2008), 248–59.

30. On the NT and Christ's priesthood, see O'Collins and Jones, *Jesus Our Priest*, 1–68.

Paul

Paul writes of the risen Christ who "intercedes for us" at the right hand of God (Rom. 8:34). Hebrews was to take this language further by characterizing the permanent intercession as Christ being "a priest forever" (7:22, 24). Without applying the title "priest" to Christ, the apostle expounds themes about Christ's priesthood and, in particular, its universal significance.[31] In Romans, immediately after establishing that "all" human beings, Jews and Gentiles alike, "have sinned and fallen short of the glory of God" (3:23), Paul introduces sacrificial, priestly imagery to present Christ as the means for wiping away the sins of humanity (3:25).[32] He then elaborately contrasts the surpassing work of Christ for human salvation with the universal effects of Adam's disobedience. Obviously using them as synonyms, the apostle passes from speaking of "all" (5:12) to speaking of "the many" (5:15), and then back to "all" (5:18) and, finally, back to "the many" (5:19). For Paul, "the many" (*polloi*) is equivalent to "all" (*pantes*). In 2 Corinthians, the apostle simply uses "all": "One has died for all, therefore all have died. And he died for all, so that those who live might live no longer for themselves" (2 Cor. 5:14–15). The priestly redemption, effected by Christ's death and resurrection, has a universal impact.

In the seven letters commonly recognized as coming directly from Paul (Romans, 1 and 2 Corinthians, Galatians, Philippians, 1 Thessalonians, and Philemon), he never speaks of Jesus specifically as priest. He attributes other titles to Jesus: above all, Christ/Messiah, Lord, and Son of God. In the first of the Pastoral Epistles (which most scholars would not attribute in their present form to Paul), Jesus is called "the one mediator between God and human beings, who gave himself as a ransom

---

31. Ibid., 27–35.
32. First John 2:2 speaks of Christ as "the means of expiating" not only "our sins" but also "the sins of the world"; on this verse and Romans 3:25, see O'Collins and Jones, *Jesus Our Priest*, 30–31.

for all" (1 Tim. 2:5).[33] The verse points us toward two other
works of the NT. First, Hebrews also calls Christ "mediator"
and does so three times when it presents his priestly work as
being that of "the mediator of the new/better covenant" (Heb.
8:6; 9:15; 12:24). Second, Mark's Gospel represents Jesus as the
Son of Man who came "to give his life as a ransom for many"
(10:45). Here "the many" is equivalent to "all" in 1 Timothy.

John

Even more than Paul, John's Gospel gets close to giving Jesus
the title of "priest" through applying to him priestly imagery
and themes.[34] In particular, the evangelist presents the high
priest (Caiaphas) as clinching the debate about killing Jesus
with words that express simultaneously "a criminal human
calculation and a divine plan of redemption."[35] What Caiaphas says enjoys prophetic value rooted in the priestly nature
of his office: "It is better to have one man die for the people
than to have the whole nation destroyed." As John comments,
these words reveal a central truth about Jesus as priest and
victim: he was about to die for the sake of and on behalf of
the whole people, and that people would include not only
Israel but also all the scattered children of God (11:49–52).
The plan of Caiaphas to do away with Jesus had unwittingly
set in motion a "universal plan of salvation to produce one
people of God."[36]

---

33. On this verse, see Luke Timothy Johnson, *The First and Second
Letters to Timothy* (New York: Doubleday, 2001), 191–92; Jerome D. Quinn
and William C. Wacker, *The First and Second Letters to Timothy* (Grand
Rapids, MI: Eerdmans, 2000), 165–66.

34. O'Collins and Jones, *Jesus Our Priest*, 24–26; Chapter 4 below will
develop further what John's Gospel suggests about the priesthood of
Christ.

35. Albert Vanhoye, *Old Testament Priests and the New Priest*
(Petersham, MA: St Bede's Publications, 1986), 14.

36. Andrew T. Lincoln, *The Gospel According to John* (London: Continuum, 2003), 330–31.

Surely this strikingly universal passage from John about Christ as priest and victim should nourish *any* Christian theology of religions. But Christ as priest and victim remains sadly absent in current theologies of religion.

Sampling the Tradition: Pius XI and *Sacrosanctum Concilium*

After sampling the NT on Christ's priesthood and its universal significance, we can investigate, albeit more briefly, how the Christian tradition understood that priesthood. Here reflections might be drawn from Augustine, other church fathers, Thomas Aquinas, Martin Luther, John Calvin, the seventeenth-century French school, John Henry Newman, and other sources. Let me limit myself to Pope Pius XI and the Second Vatican Council's Constitution on the Sacred Liturgy, *Sacrosanctum Concilium*.

Luther, among other earlier writers, had recognized an intimate association between Christ's universal kingship and priesthood.[37] The liturgy for the Feast of Christ the King, instituted by Pius XI in 1925, also makes this connection; the preface addresses God the Father as follows:

> You anointed Jesus Christ, your only Son, with the oil of gladness, as the eternal priest and universal king. *As priest* he offered his life on the altar of the cross and redeemed the human race by this one perfect sacrifice of peace. *As king* he claims dominion over all creation, so that he may present to you, his almighty Father, a universal kingdom: a kingdom of truth and life, a

---

37. O'Collins and Jones, *Jesus Our Priest*, 133–34. Alison Milbank, "Seeing Double: The Crucified Christ in Western Mediaeval Art," in Francesca A. Murphy and Troy A. Stefano (eds.), *The Oxford Handbook of Christology* (Oxford: Oxford University Press, 2015), points out that "in many early wooden crucifixes" Christ "wears the *colobium*, a priestly garment also worn by kings to show their sacerdotal role of service to their people" (215–32, at 216).

kingdom of holiness and grace, a kingdom of justice, love, and peace (italics mine).

Christ is being celebrated as king, but the preface and, to some extent, the prayer over the gifts and the prayer after communion, without any special pleading, also attend to the priesthood of Christ. If distinguishable, the kingship and priesthood of Christ are inseparable; both extend to the whole "human race" and to "all creation." The preface calls him "eternal priest" and "universal king."[38] But it could have switched the adjectives and called him "universal priest" and "eternal king." Both his priesthood and his kingship are universal in their scope and eternal in their duration.

In the first document it promulgated (December 4, 1963), Vatican II quoted (without giving the reference) a passage from Pius XII's 1947 encyclical on liturgy, *Mediator Dei*.[39] Significantly replacing "the Word of God" with a title that evokes Hebrews, *Sacrosanctum Concilium* stated: "Jesus Christ, the high priest of the new and eternal covenant, when he assumed a human nature, introduced into this land of exile the hymn that in heaven is sung throughout all ages. He unites the whole community of humankind with himself and associates it with him in singing the divine canticle of praise" (*SC* 83). Earlier the same constitution had taught that the risen Christ is present "when the church prays *and sings*" (*SC* 7; italics mine). Now the same document summed up this singing as "one divine canticle of praise," led by the incarnate, high-priestly cantor. He associates with himself not only the church but also "the whole community of humankind" in singing a heavenly hymn that he

---

38. The Nicene-Constantinopolitan Creed professes that "his [Christ's] kingdom will have no end." Hebrews 7:24 could encourage us to say: "his priesthood will have no end."

39. "The Word of God, when he assumed a human nature, introduced into this land of exile the hymn that in heaven is sung throughout all ages. He unites the whole community of humankind with himself and associates it with him in singing this divine canticle of praise" (*Mediator Dei* 144 [London: Catholic Truth Society, 1959], 58).

has brought to earth. The picture brilliantly presents Christ the high priest as joining with himself, in virtue of his incarnation, all human beings without exception, including millions who will go through life without ever hearing his name. Without consciously knowing this, they belong to his cosmic chorus and are constantly affected by his priestly work.

Christ's Priesthood and "the Others"

After sampling some items from the scriptures and tradition, how would I propose relating Christ's priesthood to the followers of other religions? What significance could that priesthood have for a theology of religions or, rather, a Christology of religions? Let me propose seven points:

(1) Christ's priesthood is made possible by his assuming a human existence (see Rahner and Hebrews above), through which he has become part (the supreme part) of creation and head of the human community.

In its Declaration on the Relation of the Church to Non-Christian Religions, the Second Vatican Council named "stemming from the one stock which God created" as the initial reason for recognizing how all human beings form one community (*NA* 1). What makes Christ's priesthood possible—namely, his created humanity— is precisely what binds him to all people of all places and times. It is that created humanity that, from the outset, constitutes him in his universal priesthood.

To be sure, the institution of the Eucharist will prove a further, decisive moment toward constituting Christ as high priest.[40] But the Eucharist *also* embodies a cosmic, universal significance that involves all human beings and the whole created world. In a lyric passage from his 2002 encyclical *Ecclesia de Eucharistia*, Pope John Paul II recalled how he had celebrated "Holy Mass in chapels built along mountain paths, on lakeshores and seacoasts. I have celebrated it on altars built

---

40. See O'Collins and Jones, *Jesus Our Priest*, 19–24, 250–61.

in stadiums and city squares. . . . This varied scenario of celebrations of the Eucharist has given me a powerful experience of its universal and, so to speak, cosmic character." Echoing a famous work by Pierre Teilhard de Chardin (1881– 1955),[41] the pope added:

> Even when it is celebrated on the humble altar of a country church, the Eucharist is always in some way celebrated *on the altar of the world*. It unites heaven and earth. It embraces and permeates all creation. The Son of God became man in order to *restore* all creation, in one supreme act of praise, to the One who made it out of nothing. He, the Eternal High Priest who by the blood of his Cross entered the eternal sanctuary, thus gives back to the Creator and Father all creation redeemed.[42]

What then "is accomplished in the Eucharist" is nothing less than "the world, which came forth from the hands of God the Creator," now returning "to him redeemed by Christ."[43] The Eucharist "embraces" all creation and hence the entire human race. Christ, the invisible minister actively present at every celebration of the Eucharist, intends to accomplish through it the redemption of all human beings, Christians and non-Christians alike.

In the passage we have just cited from John Paul II's encyclical, he did not link the priesthood of Christ with the followers of other religions. Yet to the extent that the Eucharist "embraces" the whole of creation, it involves all men and women and effectively links them to Christ the eternal high priest.

(2) From the time of Paul (1 Cor. 15 and then Rom. 5) and St. Irenaeus (in the second century), Christian theology, liturgy,

---

41. P. Teilhard de Chardin, "The Mass on the World," in *Hymn of the Universe* (London: Collins, 1965), 19–37.

42. *EE* 8, in *AAS* 95 (2003), 433–75, at 437–38; italics in original.

43. Ibid.

art, drama, and legends have associated Christ with every man and every woman through two corporate figures: the first Adam of the Genesis story and Christ as the New or Last Adam.[44]

The figures of Adam and Eve symbolize the human condition in its glory and misery. A hymn by the Latin poet Venantius Fortunatus (d. around 610), *Crux fidelis* ("faithful cross"), links two trees, the tree in the middle of the garden of Eden and the tree on Calvary, in one great drama of creation, fall, and redemption. The preface for the Feast of the Holy Cross, or Exaltation of the Cross (September 14), a feast that goes back at least to the seventh century, declares: "Death came from a tree, life was to spring from a tree." Some imaginative writers and artists have also linked Adam and the Second Adam through the symbol of gardens: from the garden of Eden, over which Adam and Eve presided, to the garden of Gethsemane, the garden where Christ was buried and after his resurrection met Mary Magdalene (John 19:41–42; 20:11–18), and, finally, the garden of the heavenly Jerusalem, which Christ as the slain and risen Lamb will illuminate (Rev. 21:23; 22:1–2). Adam and Christ featured frequently in popular medieval drama. The mystery plays highlighted the connection between the two Adams by the practice of having the same actor portray both Adam and Christ.[45]

In connecting Adam and Christ, no work of literature has surpassed "Hymn to God my God in my Sickness," written by John Donne shortly before he died:

> We think that Paradise and Calvary,
> Christ's cross and Adam's tree, stood in one place.
> Look, Lord, and find both Adams met in me;

---

44. See G. O'Collins, *Jesus Our Redeemer: A Christian Approach to Salvation* (Oxford: Oxford University Press, 2007), 37–42.

45. See further Rosemary Woolf, *The English Mystery Plays* (Berkeley: University of California Press, 1980); and Brian O. Murdoch, *Adam's Grace: Fall and Redemption in Medieval Literature* (Cambridge: D. S. Brewer, 2000).

> As the first Adam's sweat surrounds my face,
> May the last Adam's blood my soul embrace. (5.21-25)[46]

Donne recalls here an old and enduring legend that told the story of the tree from which Adam and Eve took the forbidden fruit and how it came to be used as the tree on which Christ died. According to a related legend, Calvary was the place where Adam was buried; accordingly, the Church of the Holy Sepulchre contains an "Adam Chapel." Christian artists at times placed his skull, and occasionally even his skeleton, at the foot of the cross. The New Adam died above the grave of the first Adam. Some artists pictured Adam and Eve standing together in a sarcophagus under the cross and looking up at the crucified Christ. A few representations have the figure of Adam holding a chalice to receive the first drops of blood falling from Christ on the cross.[47] The chalice symbolizes Adam's priesthood and links him (and Eve) with the defining moment in the exercise of Christ's priesthood: his death and exaltation.

One might recognize a prefiguring of this association by interpreting Adam and Eve as the priests of creation. In the "P," or Priestly, tradition, being created in the image and likeness of God and as the crown of creation, the primeval couple have "dominion" over other created beings (Gen. 1:26–31). Then follows a different tradition (often called the "J," or Yahwist, tradition) of their being created in a garden (Gen. 2:4b–25), which involves some ancient temple imagery. In this tradition, instead of being created earlier, animals and birds are

---

46. *John Donne*, ed. John Carey (Oxford: Oxford University Press, 1990), 332.

47. See Gertrud Schiller, *Iconography of Christian Art* (London: Lund Humphries, 1971), 2:131, 479. She quotes a legend about the death of Adam drawn from the Syrian *Cave of Treasures*. Apropos of Christ's death on Calvary, Adam says to Seth: "There the Word of God will come and suffer and will be crucified up there at the place where my body lies, so that my skull will be wet with his blood. And in that hour I shall be redeemed and he will bring me back to my kingdom and restore to me my priesthood and prophetic status" (131).

created after Adam and brought to him to be named. Even if the text does not explicitly call Adam a "priestly king," that can describe his responsible place in creation and the stewardship he exercises. In particular, being created in the divine image, he resembles the coming Christ and qualifies to be understood as a priestly mediator of God's original covenant with humankind. But then, in disobediently eating the fruit of the tree of knowledge of good and evil, Adam and Eve break their covenantal relationship and suffer the consequences (Gen. 3:1–24).[48]

Acknowledging priestly overtones in the creation stories colors the meeting between Adam and the New Adam. We find here a meeting between priests, one in which every man and every woman, represented by Adam and Eve, are blessed by the New or Last Adam. Such an elaboration of an Adam Christology provides a setting for recognizing how the priesthood of Christ had and continues to have its impact on the entire human race.

Eastern icons depicting Christ's passage down into the "limbo of the Fathers" and meeting with Adam and Eve—such as the sublime one in the monastery of Chora (Istanbul)—show large crowds of people standing behind them. In liberating and raising Adam and Eve, the Second Adam raises all humanity. To be sure, such icons do not expressly present Christ as the high priest, but they do not exclude reading the scene as a meeting between priests, which embodies a redemptive impact on the entire human race and the cosmos. Whatever use might be made of Eastern icons, the original priesthood of Adam (and Eve), which a fully deployed Adam Christology could incorporate, opens the way to appreciate how the exercise of Christ's

---

48. Subsequently Cain and Abel, the sons of Adam and Eve, act in a priestly way by making offerings to God (Gen. 4:1–4). The fact that their children make priestly offerings suggests something priestly about Adam and Eve. In the story of the renewed relationship between God and human beings, Noah acts in a priestly way (see O'Collins, *Salvation for All*, 8–11). That story encourages reading in a priestly key the original relationship between God and Adam (and Eve).

priesthood (and, one should add, its sacramental enactment in the Eucharist) affects every human being, whether or not they ever become aware of this.

Thus an Adam Christology, I would argue, opens up possibilities for a theology of religions, possibilities that have not yet been taken up. Dupuis moved in that direction by presenting creation as a cosmic event in which God made a universal covenant with humanity through Adam and Eve. Although the Genesis story does not explicitly speak of a covenant relationship, Dupuis followed St. Irenaeus in recognizing a covenant given to the human race under Adam. Three further covenants followed: under Noah, under Moses, and, finally and supremely, under Christ.[49] Being involved in the making of the first covenant invested Adam, the representative of the human race, with some kind of priestly character.[50] But Dupuis did not pursue that line.

(3) John Henry Newman famously incorporated something of an Adam Christology in his hymn "Firmly I believe and truly." But it is elsewhere that we should look—to a sermon by Newman on Christ's priesthood and to one of his letters that offers hints about a primordial priesthood of all human beings, a priesthood that links them with Christ the high priest.

On April 6, 1851, when Newman chose to preach on the priesthood of Christ, he dwelt on a theme dear to Luther, Christ's priestly service for sinners, and applied the theme very broadly in the light of John 1:29 ("the lamb of God who takes away the sin of the world"). "What is a priest?" Newman asked. "See how much it implies: first the need for reconciliation; it

---

49. Dupuis, *Toward a Christian Theology*, 32–33, 64, 78. Irenaeus passed over in silence other covenants: in particular, that with Abraham and Sarah (Gen. 15:1–21).

50. In the Genesis story of the great deluge and its aftermath, Noah acts in a priestly fashion by building an altar to the Lord and making an offering; then God establishes a covenant that encompasses all humanity (Gen. 8:20–9:17).

has at once to do with sin; it presupposes sin. When then our Lord is known to come as priest, see how *the whole face of the world* is changed." Newman underlined the universal character of Christ's priestly service: "The Son of God offers for *the whole world*, and that offering is himself. He who is high as eternity, whose arms stretch through infinity, is lifted up on the cross for the sins of *the world*." Here Newman was even clearer about the universal scope of the beneficiaries of Christ's priestly sacrifice. Like Hebrews, Newman took up the language about Christ being "a priest forever according to the order of Melchizedek," but, unlike Hebrews, he applied it to the permanent sacrifice of the Mass: it is not "done and over; it lasts."[51]

Two decades later, in the aftermath of the First Vatican Council's definition of papal primacy and infallibility, William Gladstone questioned whether Catholics in the United Kingdom could remain loyal to their country. In his 1874 response to the prime minister, Newman famously portrayed conscience as taking precedence over any authority, papal or secular. He expressed this precedence by using the triple office of priest, prophet, and king: "Conscience is the aboriginal Vicar of Christ, a prophet in its information, a monarch in its peremptoriness, a priest in its blessings and anathemas, and, even though the eternal priesthood throughout the Church could cease to be, in it [the human conscience] the sacerdotal principle would remain and would have a sway."[52] Here Newman presented the triple office as if it were a spiritual genetic code that preexisted any institutional structures and highlighted in particular "the sacerdotal principle" as intrinsically shaping the human spirit.

---

51. J. H. Newman, "On the Priesthood of Christ," in *Sermon Notes of John Henry Cardinal Newman 1849–1878* (London: Longmans, Green & Co., 1914), 69–70.

52. "A Letter Addressed to His Grace, the Duke of Norfolk on Occasion of Mr. Gladstone's Recent Expostulation," in J. H. Newman, *Certain Difficulties Felt by Anglicans*, in *Catholic Teaching Considered* (London: Longman, Green & Co., 1891), 2:171–378, at 248–49.

Naming the universally present human conscience a "sacerdotal principle" or "priest in its blessings and anathemas"
could lead us to take an expression from Rahner and coin a
new expression, the "sacerdotal principle" or "sacerdotal existential" in which all human beings participate. Let me explain:
Rahner famously introduced the term "supernatural existential" to describe the situation created for human freedom by
the redemptive work of Christ. Even before they freely accept
(or reject) grace, human beings are positively preconditioned
from within by the divine self-communication offered to all in
and through Christ. Hence "the expressly Christian revelation"
is "the explicit statement of the revelation of grace," which all
human beings already experience "implicitly in the depths" of
their being.[53]

Likewise, "the sacerdotal existential," adumbrated by Newman, is the priestly condition in which all human beings participate. As "the aboriginal Vicar of Christ," it is "constituted"
by the redemptive work of Christ. Through the sacerdotal existential, which is their conscience, human beings are positively
preconditioned from within to share through baptism in the
priesthood of Christ (and in his office as prophet and king).
But they already experience that priesthood in the depths of
their being and through the voice of conscience.

One might express this by saying that all human beings
are, from their conception and birth, already priests (as well
as prophets and kings/pastors). The sacerdotal existential suggests the way in which Christ's priestly work has already shaped
them even before they ever have the chance of responding to
what that work brings them in the offer of God's grace.

(4) The priesthood of Christ involved him not only in being
tried and tested but also in becoming vulnerable to lethal persecution.[54]

---

53. K. Rahner, "Anonymous Christians," *Theological Investigations*
(London: Darton, Longman & Todd, 1969), 6:390–98, at 393–94.

54. O'Collins and Jones, *Jesus Our Priest*, 248–50.

Extreme vulnerability, as the Letter to the Hebrews recognized, belonged to his job description as priest. By assuming the human condition and becoming a priest, the incarnate Son of God made himself subject to suffering and violent death (Heb. 5:7–8). Becoming a priest involved becoming a victim—a new and disturbing aspect of Christ's priesthood. This becoming personally the victim took him quite beyond the job description not only of the Levitical priests (who sacrificed animals as victims) but also of Melchizedek (who offered some bread and wine and was held up by Hebrews as foreshadowing Jesus the high priest to come). Everywhere suffering characterizes the human condition, and Christ's priestly vulnerability puts him in solidarity with every sufferer.

Christ the high priest drew near to all human beings in pain. His self-sacrificing death on Calvary between two criminals symbolized forever his solidarity with and priestly function for those who suffer and die, an identification with human pain expressed also by the criteria for the last judgment (Matt. 25:31–46). The final blessings of the kingdom will come to those who, without necessarily recognizing Christ, have met his needs in people who suffer by being hungry, thirsty, strangers, naked, sick, or imprisoned. To articulate the worldwide presence of Christ priest and victim in all who suffer, we might take further what was argued at the end of the last chapter and say: *ubi dolor, ibi Christus sacerdos et victima* (wherever there is suffering, there is Christ priest and victim).

(5) For Hebrews the death, resurrection, and glorification of Christ characterized essentially his priesthood. But this did not mean that everything that came before, above all his public ministry, was a mere prelude to the real exercise of his priesthood. His *wise teaching* during that ministry should also be recognized as priestly.

Mediating the divine revelation to people belonged (and belongs) essentially to the work of priests.[55] The role of Jesus

---

55. Ibid., 3–4, 16–17.

as preacher/teacher entered essentially into the exercise of his priesthood, as Origen, Luther, the French school, and others emphasized.[56] He continues to exercise his priesthood by being "the light of the world" and the incarnate wisdom of God.

Hence we should acknowledge the active, if mysterious, presence of Christ the priest wherever religious truth is taught in any cultures, societies, and religions. As the Second Vatican Council stated, "the precepts and doctrines" of other religions "often reflect a ray of the Truth that enlightens all people" (*NA* 2). This is to acknowledge the priestly role of Christ as universal mediator of divine revelation and wisdom. Such mediation belongs essentially to the exercise of his priesthood.

(6) In the course of exercising his priesthood the risen and exalted Christ sends the Holy Spirit into the church and the world.

In John's Gospel, Jesus says: "When the Paraclete comes whom I will send you from the Father, the Spirit of truth who proceeds from the Father, that One will bear witness to me" (John 15:26). The evangelist associates the Spirit not only with witnessing to Jesus but also with new birth and life (3:5–8; 4:10, 14; 7:37–39), with truth and teaching (14:16–17, 26; 16:13–15), and with mission and the forgiveness of sins (20:22–23). Such witnessing, giving new life, teaching the truth, and commissioning on the part of the Spirit are ongoing activities that involve a constant sending of the Spirit by the eternal high priest. Or, to put it another way, the Spirit universalizes the priestly work of Jesus. We might say: *ubi Spiritus Sanctus, ibi Christus sacerdos* (wherever there is the Holy Spirit, there is Christ the priest).[57] We return to this theme in the next chapter.

In modern times few have done more to emphasize the universal presence and activity of the Holy Spirit than John Paul II.[58] No individual and no culture or religion is simply out-

---

56. Ibid., 243–45.
57. Ibid., 265–70.
58. For details, see O'Collins, *Salvation for All*, 227–29.

side the influence of the Spirit. The Holy Spirit, sent by Christ the high priest, is incessantly active everywhere and for everyone. Our reflections on the universal presence of the Spirit should factor in the universal presence of Christ eternally exercising his priesthood.

(7) Finally, the priesthood of Christ involves eternal *intercession* for the baptized and other human beings. It is above all at the Eucharist that the crucified and risen Christ presents lovingly to the Father a self-offering on behalf of all people. Through the power of the Holy Spirit, he draws into his own self-offering the church's intercession for the world. We will return to this theme at greater length in Chapter 4.

Here then are seven systematic ways of thinking about the followers of other faiths and indeed of all human beings, ways that draw inspiration from the priesthood of Jesus Christ. Like his kingship, that priesthood has no limits and will have no end. It throws much light on the situation and destiny of those who follow other faiths or who follow none. Yet so far in the theology of religions, the universal priesthood of Christ has remained an untold story. The theology of religions, better called the Christology of religions, would, I believe, be greatly enriched by incorporating "the sacerdotal principle" or "sacerdotal existential" that honors the priestly activity of Christ for the good of all human beings.

3

The Universal Presence of Christ
and the Holy Spirit

A Christology of the religions is unthinkable unless it encompasses the universal presence of the crucified and risen Christ and of the Holy Spirit. In the second century of the Christian era, Irenaeus of Lyons recognized the universal scope of the divine action through Christ for human salvation: "The Word of the all-powerful God . . . on the invisible plane is co-extensive with the whole of creation," "rules the universe," and as the Son of God "has traced the sign of the cross on everything" (*Demonstratio* 34). In the third century, Origen also highlighted this universal, saving presence: "Christ is so powerful that, although invisible because of his divinity, he is *present to every person* and extends over the whole universe" (*In Ioannem* 6.15; italics mine). This was not to deny that Christ is present in a special, fuller way in the lives of the baptized. But that fuller presence does not mean an absence elsewhere.

Many centuries later, St. John Paul II (1920–2005) said something similar, while letting the theme of the Holy Spirit shape the way he expressed matters. He proclaimed that the full means of salvation are available for the followers of Christ. But this faith does not entail denying the Spirit's powerful presence everywhere. As John Paul II wrote in his 1990 encyclical *Redemptoris Missio* (the Mission of the Redeemer), the universal "*presence and activity*" of the Spirit "affect not only individuals but also society and history, peoples, cultures, *and religions*"

(*RM* 28; italics mine).[1] Through the Spirit's powerful presence, "the others" participate in their own ways in the one divine plan for human salvation. We return below to the teaching of this encyclical.

In their different ways Irenaeus, Origen, and John Paul II suggest that presence, and its varieties offer the key for thinking about how divine salvation reaches all people. We live in a "world of grace,"[2] a world in which the risen and exalted Christ powerfully demonstrates his personal presence not only for the baptized but also for all "others," and does so through the Holy Spirit. A Christology of religions involves a pneumatology of religions, and vice versa. In both cases we deal with an active and universal presence.

A Christology of Universal Presence

As much or even more than anyone else, Gabriel Marcel (1889–1973) highlighted the differing qualities and modes of presence.[3] The relationships involved seem endlessly various: interpersonal presence can always be closer, more intense, more freely chosen, and more productive of an ever-closer communion of life. A seemingly endless variety of form and intensity characterizes the presences we experience: "presence" is a radically analogous term and reality. We never face a

---

1. In *Nova et Vetera* 13 (2015): 837–73, at 861, Eduardo Echeverria maintains that "God's grace may reach individuals despite but not through their religions." It is hard to reconcile this claim with the teaching of John Paul II about the Holy Spirit affecting religions—not to mention what Vatican II's Declaration on the Relation of the Church to Non-Christian Religions said about the "true and holy" elements in other religions (*Nostra Aetate* 2). See n. 7 below and G. O'Collins,"Vatican II on the Religions: A Response," *Nova et Vetera* 15 (2017): 1243–49.

2. See Leo J. O'Donovan (ed.), *A World of Grace: An Introduction to the Themes and Foundations of Karl Rahner's Theology* (New York: Seabury Press, 1980).

3. On presence and its varieties, see G. Marcel, *Homo Viator* (London: Victor Gollancz, 1951), and G. Marcel, *The Mystery of Being*, 2 vols. (London: Harvill Press, 1950–51).

simple alternative: presence or absence. It is always a question of what kind of presence and what kind of absence, or how someone is present or how someone is absent. Every presence, short of the beatific vision in the final encounter with God, is always tinged with absence.

Given the stunning variety and qualitative differences that characterize human presence, we should be ready to acknowledge an endless variety in the qualitatively different possibilities in the presence and activity of Christ and the Spirit. To allege anything less would be strangely at odds with the loving freedom of an infinitely creative God. It seems weirdly arrogant to claim limited possibilities in the case of divine presence and activity. Let us now turn to examine the strikingly new modes of divine presence to humanity and the world that the missions of the Son and the Holy Spirit involved. Let me sketch seven aspects of Christ's enduring presence in the lives of all human beings, whether Christians, adherents of other living faiths, or followers of no religious faith at all.

The universal presence of Christ is implied by: (1) the kingdom of God; (2) the Christology of Paul; (3) the doctrine of Christ as the pervasive Word or Wisdom of God; (4) the solidarity of the incarnate Logos with all (suffering) human beings; (5) Christ's resurrection from the dead, which brought a new, universal, light-giving, and life-giving presence; (6) Christ's image of himself as a mother hen and the tradition of Christ our Mother (Julian of Norwich), which encourage us to accept a universal, maternal presence; and (7) the final future of resurrected existence, which will involve the most intense union with the glorious Christ of all who are saved.

The Kingdom of God

The previous chapter expounded something of the earthly Jesus' activity for the kingdom of God. The historical Jesus, implicitly but clearly, proclaimed himself to be inseparably connected with the divine kingdom that was breaking into the world. He was and remains the kingdom in person, the *auto-*

basileia, as Origen put it (*In Matthaeum* 14.7). With and through Jesus' personal presence (in his life, death, resurrection, and ascension), the rule of God has become already present and will come in its fullness at the end of world history. Since the kingdom of God touches everyone, the revealing and saving presence of Christ, the heart of the kingdom, must do likewise. Human beings, whether they are aware of this or not, cannot escape living in the presence of Christ and coming under his influence as the kingdom of God in person.

The Christology of Paul

Joining Paul in identifying Christ as the Second or Last Adam (Rom. 5:12–21; 1 Cor. 15:22, 45–49) means acknowledging him as present to and related with all men and women, whoever they may be and wherever they may be. Just as all humanity was harmed by the sin of Adam and Eve, so the redemption brought by Christ the Last Adam has a radical impact on the entire human race and the whole created world. Likewise acknowledging him to be the reconciler of "the world" (2 Cor. 5:19; Col. 1:20), the divine agent of creation and new creation (1 Cor. 8:6), and exalted Lord of the universe (1 Cor. 15:24–28; Phil. 2:10–11) entails recognizing his all-pervasive presence and activity in the whole created world. That Pauline language rules out imagining any situation "outside Christ" (*extra Christum*). The risen Lord is an active cosmic presence. To say less would be incompatible with the faith in him articulated magisterially by Paul.[4]

Christ as the Word or Wisdom of God

From the time of Justin Martyr (d. around 165), the church fathers, such as Athanasius (see Chap. 1 above), regularly identified Christ as the divine Logos (Word) or Wisdom, who, by creating and sustaining the world, intimately accompanies

---

4. See G. O'Collins, *Salvation for All: God's Other Peoples* (Oxford: Oxford University Press, 2008), 122–28.

everyone and everything. They understood the Logos to per-
meate the body of the world. No place or person lies "far"
from God's creative Logos or Wisdom. He remains universally present.

When explaining this universal presence and its varieties,
Justin and Irenaeus portrayed the Logos as the unique source
of religious knowledge—a knowledge shared in differently by
Christians, Jews, and others. According to Justin, on the one
hand, "the seeds of the Word" are everywhere and in every
person (*Second Apology* 8.1; 13.5). On the other hand, even
though "the whole human race shares" in the Logos (*First Apology* 46.2), some people live only "according to a fragment of the
Logos." Christians live "according to the knowledge and contemplation of the whole Logos, who is Christ" (*Second Apology*
8.3). One can translate this language in terms of the endless
variety and modes not only of the presence of the Logos but
also of the knowledge that he communicates.

At the start of Chapter 1, we recalled what Athanasius wrote
in the fourth century about the universal, deifying impact of
the Word or Wisdom of God. Two centuries earlier Irenaeus
had summed up the Son's universal role in revelation as follows: "From the beginning the Son reveals (*revelat*) the Father
to all whom the Father desires, at the time and in the manner desired by the Father" (*Adversus Haereses* 4.6.7). No one is
left out when the Son discloses the Father. Yet the timing and
manner for this universal revelatory activity depend on God
and not on human beings. What matters *primarily* is God's
searching for all human beings through the Son rather than
any human search for God. As Irenaeus put matters, "no one
can know God, unless God teaches: that is, without God, God
cannot be known" (4.6.4).

Salvation belongs inseparably to this revealing activity of
the universally present Son/Logos. We quoted above a key passage from Irenaeus: "the Word of the all-powerful God . . . on
the invisible plane is co-extensive with the whole of creation,"
"rules the universe," and as Son of God "has traced the sign
of the cross on everything" (*Demonstratio* 34). While Irenaeus

held that in every part of the world the Son has in one way or another revealed the Father to all people, he knew that this universal revelatory activity involved salvation for the non-baptized. The Son, he wrote, "came to save all" (*Adversus Haereses* 2.22.4; see 2.18.7 and 4.22.2).

Solidarity of the Incarnate Logos with Humanity

The incarnation, when the Logos became flesh, enlarged his revealing and saving presence. This event put Christ into a material solidarity with all human beings and their world. Present now in a bodily, human fashion, he offered and offers new possibilities for mutual, interpersonal relationships.

He drew near to all human beings and, in a particular way, to their sufferings. His new presence made him fatally vulnerable; it cost him his life. The body of Christ on the cross expressed for all time his mysterious but truly redeeming presence to those who suffer anywhere and at any time. His death on Calvary between two criminals symbolized and revealed forever his close solidarity with those who suffer and die. To convey the worldwide presence of the crucified Christ in all who suffer, we could say: *ubi dolor, ibi Christus crucifixus* ("where there is suffering, there is Christ crucified").

When addressing the Jewish community of Vienna on June 24, 1988, John Paul II said: "Faith teaches us that God never forsakes those who suffer persecution but *reveals himself to them and enlightens through them* all peoples on the road to salvation."[5] We will return to this revelatory value of suffering in Chapter 5 below.

The Resurrection

Christ's resurrection from the dead introduced a new, universal, life-giving sharing in his presence. This post-Easter presence is reflected in Luke's preference for the language of

---

5. *AAS* 81 (1989): 218–21, at 219.

life when speaking of the resurrected Christ (e.g. Luke 24:5, 23; Acts 1:3), and in John's subsequent identification of Jesus with life itself (e.g. John 11:25; 14:6). Risen from the dead, Christ is actively present everywhere as the source of eternal life for everyone. This new presence means that Christ was not merely *with us* (through the creation and incarnation) and *for us* (through his ministry and crucifixion) but also *in us*, inviting us to respond to his intimate presence (Col. 1:27).

This personal self-bestowal, made possible through a glorious transformation that lifted the risen Christ beyond the normal limits of space and time, has effected a presence that John typically describes as "Christ-in-us" and "we-in-Christ," and Paul as "we-in-Christ." Where John's Gospel represents the new presence as a mutual indwelling, Paul usually depicts it as our dwelling "in Christ" as in a corporate personality.[6] In an unprecedented way, the risen Christ, through the Holy Spirit, enables all human beings to share in his saving presence and live "in him." This presence is real and effective but need not be a felt presence. It can remain a hidden presence—throughout the lives of innumerable human beings.

This new saving presence differs according to one's location in the world of various cultures and religions. For the baptized, the church's worship, teaching, and whole life serve to bring forth the living presence of the risen Christ. The church provides the visible verification of his invisible but actively real presence. Whenever the sacraments are administered, the risen Christ is personally and effectively present. In commenting on John's Gospel, Augustine summed up this sacramental ministry and presence of the risen Lord: "When Peter baptizes, it is Christ who baptizes. When Paul baptizes, it is Christ who baptizes. When Judas baptizes, it is Christ who baptizes" (*In Ioannem* 6.7).

In other cultures and religions the risen Christ is also redemptively present in varying ways and degrees. To echo

---

6. Occasionally Paul varies his normal usage and writes of "Christ/ Jesus in us/me" (e.g. Gal. 2:20).

Irenaeus, Christ's invisible and powerful presence is spread everywhere. In other religions, he is somehow actively "there," even before any contact with the gospel message has taken place. Vatican II's Declaration on the Relation of the Church to Non-Christian Religions observed that "the Catholic Church rejects nothing of those things which are *true and holy* in these [other] religions."[7] Rather, "it is with sincere respect that she considers those ways of acting and living, those precepts and doctrines, which, although they differ in many [aspects] from what she herself holds and proposes, nevertheless, often reflect a ray of that Truth [upper case], which illuminates all human beings" (*NA* 2; italics mine). By recognizing what is "true and holy" in other religions, this declaration uses a Johannine, double-sided terminology that distinguishes (but does not separate) the two dimensions of the divine self-communication: revelation and salvation. What or rather who has given rise to "those things that are true and holy" in other religions?

Without condemning any of the various "ways of acting and living," or any of the various "precepts and doctrines" to be found in other religions, but simply saying that they "differ" in many respects from what the Catholic Church "teaches and proposes," the declaration then acknowledges something extraordinarily positive: the beliefs and practices of other religions "often reflect a ray of that Truth which illuminates all human beings" (John 1:9).[8] Since what is "true" among the others reflects the "Truth" who is the Word of God, presumably what is holy among them also comes from the Word who is the life of humankind (John 1:4). If Christ is somehow "the truth"

---

7. *NA* speaks of "the things which are true and holy" in other "religions," and not merely in the individual followers of these other religions. Those who claim that followers of other religions can be saved *despite* their religion have serious difficulty in accommodating this teaching of the declaration.

8. The evangelist also recognizes clearly that people can resist and reject this truth and light (John 1:9, 10–11): "the light has come into the world, and people loved darkness rather than light because their deeds were evil" (John 3:19).

offered to everyone, he is also somehow "the life" offered to them. This paragraph from *Nostra Aetate* does not expressly state that Christ functions as both the universal revealer and universal savior, but what it says amounts to this. How can he seek to "illuminate" everybody without also seeking to convey to them something of God's self-revelation and hence also the offer of salvation?

A year before *Nostra Aetate* appeared in 1965, *Lumen Gentium* said of morally upright atheists, agnostics, and perhaps also of "God-seekers" in general: "Whatever good or truth is found among them is considered by the church to be a preparation for the gospel, and given by him [Christ] who *enlightens* all human beings so that they may at length have *life*" (*LG* 16; italics mine). *Nostra Aetate* took matters further by referring the paired blessings ("true and holy") and the enlightenment by the Word specifically to Hindus, Buddhists, and followers of "other religions" (*NA* 2). Here the light of Christ is explicitly linked with the life he offers. The incarnate and risen Christ interacts with the whole world, albeit in ways that are different. He is absent from nobody, but interacts differently with everybody.

Beyond question, this Christian affirmation may seem to many "others" an appalling piece of arrogance. They give their allegiance to other religions or to none at all and will resist claims about Jesus present everywhere and lovingly interacting with everyone. Yet we should recall three points. First, this claim is personal and not institutional; it maintains the universal impact of Jesus himself and not of the Christian church as such. (We come to the church in the next chapter.) Second, we should not forget that some other religions (e.g. Islam and certain forms of Hinduism) honor Christ and include him in one way or another in their faith. They may not endorse the universal significance of Christ that is proposed here, but they certainly do not deny all significance to him. Third, while Christians should not ignore the claims of other religions, they should not play down or misrepresent their own claims about Jesus universally present to mediate salvation and revelation everywhere. In my experience, adherents of other faiths find such dissimulation, even when adopted by Christians for "the best of reasons," dishonest and even disrespectful toward partners in interreligious dialogue.

Maternal Images of Christ

Jesus applied to himself a homely, feminine image: he was present like a mother hen to shelter her chickens when they run back under her wings (Luke 13:34 par.). Recalling this picture of Jesus as mother hen, Augustine drew on an ancient legend about the pelican, who sheds her blood over her dead offspring and so dies by bringing them back to life (*Enarrationes in Psalmos* 102.8). Augustine encouraged later writers (and artists) to take up the image of Christ as "the loving pelican" who died for all people (see 2 Cor. 5:14).

The maternal images of hen and pelican could encourage us to find a plus value in Paul's (or rather Luke's) language of God as the One "in whom we live and move and have our being" (Acts 17:28). During the first nine months of our existence, we each live, move, and have our being within our mother, on whom we radically depend for life, sustenance, and growth. This image may be applied to the risen Christ, whose all-encompassing presence forms the "place" where all members of the human race, including those who do not or do not yet acknowledge explicitly his presence, live and move and have their being.

Julian of Norwich expressed this presence as follows: "Jesus is in all who will be saved, and all who will be saved are in Jesus."[9] This sense of mutual indwelling went hand in hand with Julian's wonderful sense of "Christ our Mother."[10]

---

9. Julian of Norwich, *Showings*, chap. 51 (New York: Paulist Press, 1976), 276.

10. She claimed a wonderful paradox when she wrote: "Our Savior is our true Mother, in whom we are endlessly born and out of whom we shall never come" (ibid., chap. 57, 292).

The Final Future of Resurrected Existence

Thus far I have been articulating the relationship between the incarnate and risen Christ and those who have not or have not yet heard the message about him. At the end of history, a supreme form of self-bestowal will bring, for all those who are saved, an eternal communion of life and love through a qualitatively supreme form of his presence. Christ's rising from the dead has already initiated the presence of the end. But with his final coming human beings and their world will be raised and transformed (1 Cor. 15:20–28).

We may give this vision of the final future further shape by invoking the bodily character of presence. Christ is already "there" for us, whenever we encounter the body of the created world, various embodiments of the kingdom of God, all human bodies (especially of those who suffer), the body of the church, and the body of world religions. "Every body" and everybody mediate his presence here and now in an innumerable variety of ways and with varying degrees of clarity and intensity. At the consummation of all things, everyone and everything will be drawn together in his glorious body to enjoy the unconditional divine hospitality that is eternal life.

Augustine was second to none when it came to envisaging the final presence of all in Christ. He summoned the faithful to their future life: "be united in him [Christ] alone, be one reality alone, be one person alone" (*in uno estote, unum estote, unus estote*) (*In Ioannem* 12.9). From the incorporation of all in Christ, Augustine moved to a profound solidarity with him, and even to a personal assimilation. Augustine, while expounding and defending the resurrection of individuals to eternal life, also insisted on their being drawn in the closest imaginable way into the presence of Christ: "and there will be one Christ loving himself" (*et erit unus Christus amans seipsum*) (*In Primam Epistolam Ioannis* 10.3).

Augustine also expressed the final communion of life in the divine presence through the theme of praise: "there we shall praise, we shall all be one, in him [Christ] who is One, oriented towards the One [the Father]; for then, although many, we shall not be scattered" (*ibi laudabimus, omnes unus in uno ad unum erimus*; *quia deinceps multi dispersi non erimus*; *Enarrationes in Psalmos* 147.28). Addressing the triune God, Augustine also said: "and without ceasing we shall say one thing, praising You [the Trinity] in unison, even ourselves being also made one in You [the Trinity]" (*et sine fine dicemus unum laudantes te in unum, et in te facti etiam nos unum*; *De Trinitate* 15.28.51).

The last chapter recalled how the first document to issue from Vatican II introduced the "one divine canticle of praise," led by the high-priestly cantor: "Jesus Christ, the high priest of the new and eternal covenant, when he assumed a human nature, introduced into this land of exile the hymn that in heaven is sung throughout all the ages. He unites *the whole community of humankind* with himself and associates it with him in singing the divine canticle of praise" (*SC* 83; italics mine). The "canticle of praise" is presumably directed to God the Father, and is understood to be a hymn sung by all creatures in heaven. Christ in his priestly role is represented as having inaugurated the singing of the divine praises on earth by assuming the human condition in his incarnation. He is pictured as joining not merely those who come to know and believe in him but also the whole human community to himself in a chorus, of which he is obviously the leader. This passage strikingly portrays the active presence of Christ to all human beings. This unity of the entire human race in him,[11] which began with the incarnation, must be understood to be strengthened and perfected through the resurrection and coming of the Holy Spirit. Finally, it will be consummated when human beings reach "the halls of heaven." This picture of Christ the cosmic choir master serves brilliantly to symbolize the union in him of all, baptized and nonbaptized alike. Long before they become aware of this, even those who have never heard his name are mysteriously but truly in the hands of Christ the choir master of the world.

---

11. Thomas Aquinas called Christ "the head of all human beings," albeit "in different degrees" (*Summa Theologiae* IIIa.83 ad 1).

A Pneumatology of Universal Presence

Centuries ago Spanish navigators gave the island continent of Australia a beautiful name: "the land of the Holy Spirit." Not only Australia but also the entire planet could be called "the land of the Holy Spirit." Everywhere present, the Spirit gives life and growth to everyone and everything, and in doing so brings them to Christ.[12]

On the one hand, the universal presence of the Holy Spirit enacts and accompanies the presence of the risen Christ, which is therefore also a universal presence. On the other hand, since the co-sender of the Spirit (the risen Christ) is always inseparably there with the sent (the Holy Spirit) and since Christ is present everywhere and in every human life, the Spirit must also be present everywhere and in every human life. Yet people—and, specifically, those who follow "other" faiths—do not have to be aware of living in the presence of Christ and the Holy Spirit for this to be the case. *Being present* does not necessarily imply *being known to be present.* Let us recall the witness to the Spirit's universal presence and activity coming from three modern writers (Ingolf Dalferth, Henry Edward Manning, and John V. Taylor), the Second Vatican Council, and John Paul II.

Since the Christ and his Spirit are present everywhere and to everyone, they cannot fail to act everywhere and do so lovingly toward all. As Dalferth has written, they exercise their divine love "in an infinite series of unique acts of love, each new and different from all the others."[13] But Christ and the Spirit do not necessarily and always make their presence consciously felt. It is, in any case, a matter of common experience that "we experience many things without knowing *what* we experience or *how* we experience them."[14] To this one can add that we can expe-

---

12. On the Holy Spirit, see G. O'Collins, *The Tripersonal God: Understanding and Interpreting the Trinity,* 2nd ed. (Mahwah, NJ: Paulist Press, 2014), 165–73.

13. I. Dalferth, *Becoming Present: An Inquiry into the Christian Sense of the Presence of God* (Leuven: Peeters, 2006), 147.

14. Ibid., 115; italics mine.

rience personal agents without necessarily knowing *whom* we experience. We may never, for instance, know the identity of some mysterious stranger who proves particularly helpful to us. While being the primary agent for the life and mission of the church, the Holy Spirit *also* works to transform everyone and everything in the world. Baptism, the Eucharist, and other outward signs of the church's life do not circumscribe and limit the operations of the Spirit. In its invisible mission the Spirit offers everyone the possibility of being changed by the saving grace of Christ's dying and rising from the dead.[15] The Spirit communicates life to everyone and illuminates the journey of all humanity toward God, a pilgrimage that will bring human beings everywhere to make up the one body of Christ.

One modern but often neglected witness to the universal mission of the Holy Spirit was Cardinal Henry Edward Manning (1808–92). He wrote:

> It is true to say with St. Irenaeus, "*ubi ecclesia ibi Spiritus* (where the Church is, there is the Spirit)," but it would not be true to say, "where the Church is not, neither is the Spirit there." The operations of the Holy Ghost have always pervaded the whole race of men from the beginning, and they are now in full activity, even among those who are without the Church.[16]

In the twentieth century, Bishop John V. Taylor recognized the full extent of the universal mission of the Spirit, or "the Go-Between God," who acts as a kind of divine broker, subtly reaching everywhere and creating true relationships. The Holy Spirit, he wrote, is "that unceasing, dynamic communicator

---

15. In the words of Vatican II's Pastoral Constitution on the Church in the Modern World (*Gaudium et Spes*), "since Christ died for all and since human beings have in fact one and the same final calling, namely a divine one, we ought to hold that the Holy Spirit offers to all the possibility of being united, in a way known to God, to the paschal mystery" (*GS* 22).

16. H. E. Manning, *The Internal Mission of the Holy Ghost* (New York: P. J. Kenedy, 1875), v.

and Go-Between operating upon every element and every process of the material universe, the immanent and anonymous presence of God"—in short, the "creative-redemptive action at the heart of everything."[17]

Footnote 15 above quoted some words about the universal impact of the Holy Spirit from an article in *Gaudium et Spes* that Pope John Paul II repeatedly cited.[18] But this constitution had much more to say about the Holy Spirit affecting the whole of humanity: for instance, its teaching that "Christ, who died and was raised for all, will *through his Spirit* give life and strength to human beings so that they can respond to their supreme calling" (*GS* 10; italics mine). Indeed, "the people of God believes" that "the Spirit of the Lord fills the whole world" (*GS* 11). Observing how an awareness of "the supreme dignity" of human persons and their "universal rights and duties" has been growing in the whole world, *Gaudium et Spes* stated: "the Spirit of God, who with wonderful providence directs the march of time and renews the face of the earth, assists at this evolution." This was to assign to the Holy Spirit a leading role in the development toward a social order "founded on truth, built on justice, and enlivened by love" (*GS* 26).

Some of this teaching from Vatican II links up directly with the central scope of this book. To maintain, for example, that the Spirit gives all human beings the "light and strength" they need to fulfill their divinely given vocation is tantamount to saying that the Holy Spirit gives to all, whatever the faith by which they live, the revealing light and saving strength that they need if they are to enjoy through the risen Christ eternal life with God.

Here a relevant piece of teaching from St. Paul on the impact of the Holy Spirit came into its own with the teaching of

---

17. J. V. Taylor, *The Go-Between God* (London: SCM Press, 1972), 64.

18. See H.-J. Sander, "Die Gravitationszentrum des Lehramtes von Papst Johannes Paul II in GS 22," in P. Hünermann and B. J. Hilberath (eds.), *Herders Theologischer Kommentar zum Zweiten Vatikanischen Konzil* (Freiburg im Breisgau: Herder, 2005), 4:859–61.

John Paul II: "no one can say 'Jesus is Lord' except by the Holy Spirit" (1 Cor. 12:3). In the context of the letter, the apostle was perhaps offering advice on discerning episodes of ecstatic prayer. The Corinthians could be sure that those who cried out "Jesus is the Lord" did so under the impulse of the Holy Spirit. Or possibly Paul referred to a very brief "credo" professed on the occasion of baptism. But it seems more likely that he had in mind a public confession made in times of persecution. Through the agency of the Spirit believers were empowered to confess Jesus as "my/our/the Lord" (see Matt. 10:17–19), rather than apostatize and declare under pressure that "Jesus is cursed" or "cursed is the Lord."[19]

When commenting on this passage in the fourth century, an anonymous author who eventually came to be distinguished from Ambrose of Milan and known as "Ambrosiaster" wrote: "whatever truth is said by anyone is said by the Holy Spirit" (*quidquid enim verum, a quocumque dicitur, a Sancto dicitur Spiritu*).[20] In the form of "everything that is true, no matter by whom it is said, is from the Holy Spirit" (*omne verum, a quocumque dicatur, a Spiritu Sancto est*), the statement turned up eighteen times in the works of Thomas Aquinas.[21] In the late twentieth century, John Paul II gave the principle a fresh twist that put it back in the original context of prayer, albeit authentic prayer that can go up to God anywhere and not simply prayer uttered within a meeting of ecstatically gifted Christians. Let me explain.

In his 1979 encyclical *Redemptor Hominis* (the Redeemer of the Human Person), John Paul supported "coming closer together with representatives of the non-Christian religions" through "dialogue, contacts, and *prayer in common*" (*RH* 6;

---

19. See Joseph A. Fitzmyer, *First Corinthians* (New Haven, CT: Yale University Press, 2008), 455–56, 459–60; Anthony C. Thiselton, *The First Letter to the Corinthians* (Grand Rapids, MI: Eerdmans, 2000), 916–17.

20. *In Epistolam B. Pauli ad Corinthios Primam* 12,3; Patrologia Latina 17, col. 245B; the passage is also found in CSEL 81, pars. 2,132.

21. E.g. *Summa Theologiae* II-II, q. 172, a. 6 arg. 1. Like others, Thomas believed that the saying came from Ambrose of Milan.

italics mine). In October 1986 he boldly broke new ground by doing just that; he went off to Assisi with the Dalai Lama and other heads or representatives of the world's religions to pray for peace. Some Catholics, including members of the Roman Curia, judged harshly the event in Assisi as if it betrayed Christian faith in Jesus. The pope answered his critics in his Christmas address to the Roman Curia, delivered on December 22, 1986. He echoed and adapted the dictum of Ambrosiaster and Aquinas to speak not of truth but of prayer: "every authentic prayer is called forth by the Holy Spirit." For good measure, he added that the Spirit "is mysteriously present in the heart of every person."[22] That same year the universal activity of the Holy Spirit had already firmly entered papal teaching.

John Paul II dedicated a long encyclical letter, *Dominum et Vivificantem* (Lord and Giver of Life), published at Pentecost 1986, to the Holy Spirit, active in the life of the church and in the whole world. According to God's plan of salvation, the "action" of the Spirit "has been exercised in every place and at every time, indeed in every individual"—an action that, to be sure, is "closely linked with the mystery of the incarnation and the redemption" (*DV* 5). That is to say, the universal activity of the Spirit is inseparably connected with what the Son of God did for all human beings by taking on the human condition, by dying and rising from the dead, and by sending the gift of the Holy Spirit from the Father. While endorsing a universal activity of the Holy Spirit, the pope also acknowledged that "the marvelous 'condescension' of the Spirit *meets with resistance and opposition* in our human reality" (*DV* 55; emphasis original). The grace of the Spirit can be resisted and rejected by human beings.

At the start of this chapter we recalled another encyclical, *Redemptoris Missio* of 1990. There John Paul II insisted that,

---

22. *AAS* 79 (1987): 1082–90, at 1089. The text of the address was fully published by the Secretariat of Non-Christians (renamed in 1988 the Pontifical Council for Interreligious Dialogue), *Bulletin* 64/22/1 (1987): 54–62. The key passages are found in ND 1949–52.

while manifested "in a special way in the Church and her members," the Spirit's "presence and activity" are, nevertheless, "universal." He understood the Spirit to operate "at the very source" of each human person's "religious questioning." He went on to say: "the Spirit's presence and activity affect not only individuals but also society and history, peoples, *cultures and religions*" (*RM* 28; italics mine). Two momentous statements came into play here.

First of all, the Holy Spirit actively operates in and through the questions that sooner or later arise for everyone: Where did I come from? Where am I going? What is the meaning of life? What do suffering, sin, and evil mean? What will come after death? Who is the God in whom I live and move and have my being (Acts 17:28)? As far as John Paul II was concerned, the Holy Spirit is actively present and operating not only whenever anyone prays authentically but also whenever anyone faces the profound religious questions of life. One might coin a new dictum along the lines of Ambrosiaster and Aquinas: "Every truly religious question, no matter by whom it is raised, is from the Holy Spirit" (*omnis quaestio vere religiosa, a quocumque moveatur, a Spiritu Sancto est*). No human being exists outside the powerful presence of God the Holy Spirit. The Spirit is the mysterious companion and religious friend who raises deep and necessary questions in the life of every human being. When we share this picture, we are not too far from the way in which Luke in Acts 17 describes Paul engaging the Athenians through their questions and desire to know.

Second, John Paul II appreciated how the presence and activity of the Holy Spirit also affect the wider human society and all human "history, peoples, cultures, and religions." The Spirit acts through the cultures and religious traditions of our world. This activity is inseparable from the salvation that the crucified and risen Christ has brought about. It is an activity aimed at bringing all people, sooner or later, to Christ. In the meantime, the Spirit is present and operative in and through all that is true, good, and beautiful in various cultures and religions around the world.

This vision of the universal presence of the Holy Spirit requires a rich view of the nature of personal presence. We should never think in terms of a sharp alternative, as if the Spirit were either totally present or completely absent. That would be to ignore the vast variety of ways in which personal agents are present. Personal presence can assume many forms and exhibit great differences in intensity. What is true between human beings holds all the more true of the innumerable variety of ways in which the Holy Spirit is present to human beings, both as individuals and in their different cultures and religious traditions. To be sure, the Spirit is present in a quite special and intense way within the Christian church. But, as Henry Manning warned, that does not allow us to say: "outside the church there is no Holy Spirit." In fact, there is no such situation as being "outside the Spirit." No place, person, culture, or religion is simply "outside" the Holy Spirit. We need here a broad vision of presence—in particular, of that active presence of the Spirit that can assume indefinitely many modalities and intensities.

Conclusion

This chapter has adopted the language of "presence" to throw some light on the mysterious activity of the risen Christ and of the Holy Spirit whose love unites people everywhere to the one Christ.[23] Characteristically, Paul pictured the life of Christians as their being "in Christ" and as the Holy Spirit being "in them." Unless we rigidly insist that "one size fits all" and that this "being in" can come only in one shape or form, there is ample room left to acknowledge that the Holy Spirit is also "in" those who have never been baptized and that these non-baptized can also in some real sense "be in Christ." This all-pervasive presence embodies the love of Christ and the Spirit

---

23. See David V. Meconi, *The One Christ*: *St. Augustine's Theology of Deification* (Washington, DC: Catholic University of America Press, 2013), 165–72.

for each and every human being; for such presence is inconceivable without factoring in their active relationship of love. The next chapter will take up some aspects of this love.

This book began by spelling out a Christology of religions in terms of Christ himself. Since there can be no satisfactory Christology without a pneumatology, it moved to the inseparable Holy Spirit. In other words, a Christology of religions entails a trinitarian perspective. The mission of the Son and the mission of the Spirit merge in leading all people home to God the Father.

What would such a Christology of the religions indicate about the community of the baptized, the Christian church herself joined to Christ her head and held together by the Holy Spirit? This question leads us now to a relevant theme in ecclesiology: the church's intercession for "the others."

4

The Church Joins Christ in Loving Intercession for All People

Since the time of Pope Pius XII, the relationship between those of other faiths (or of no faith at all) and baptized Christians has often been expressed in terms of "the others" being "oriented" toward the church. His 1943 encyclical *Mystici Corporis Christi* wrote of those who do not belong to the Catholic Church but are "oriented toward [it] by a certain unconscious desire and wish."[1] Without referring to this encyclical, Vatican II's Dogmatic Constitution on the Church used the same verb when teaching that "those who have not yet received the gospel are oriented (*ordinantur*) toward the Church in various ways" (*LG* 16).

But why not reverse direction and examine how the Christian church is oriented toward those of other living faiths (or of no particular faith at all), in particular through prayers of intercession for them? The Second Vatican Council in the Decree on the Church's Missionary Activity encouraged bishops "to raise up among their people, especially among those who are sick and afflicted with hardships, souls who with an open heart will offer prayers and works of penance to God for the evangelization of the world" (*AG* 38). The same decree notes how prayers offered by contemplative religious enjoy "the greatest importance," since it is in answer to prayer that "God sends

---

1. *Mystici Corporis Christi* 103 and *AAS* 35 (1943): 233.

workers into his harvest (Matt. 9:38), opens the minds of non-Christians to hear the gospel (Acts 16:14), and makes the word of salvation fruitful in their hearts (1 Cor. 3:7)" (*AG* 40). Does such intercession, by sharing in the high priestly function of Christ, constitute a mediation of salvation and shed light on the Christology of religions? So far this question of prayer has hardly been raised in the theology of religions, and those who have raised it have not attended to (a) the rich teaching on the prayer of intercession provided by the Christian tradition right down to the present day; or to (b) the effective love that inspires such intercession; or to (c) the eternal priesthood of Christ that this intercession participates in—a theme to which we have already dedicated a chapter and which belongs preeminently to a Christology of religions. Before attending to themes (a), (b), and (c), let us recall how prayer has so far entered the discussion.

Francis Sullivan

In a 1992 book, Francis Sullivan proposed that in praying for all humanity, the church plays an "instrumental role in the salvation of a great number of people" whom it "does not reach" with "word or sacrament." The "priestly people" exercises this "mediating role" when offering the Eucharist "not only for the Christian faithful, but [also] for the salvation of the whole world." In support of his position, Sullivan cited passages from the Third and Fourth Eucharistic Prayers that include such prayers for the salvation of all humanity.[2]

While appealing to the Eucharist and the priestly role of all who participate, Sullivan said nothing, however, either about Vatican II's restoration of the Prayer of the Faithful (which prescribes praying "for all human beings and for the salvation of the entire world"[3]) or about the love that motivates interceding

---

2. F. A. Sullivan, *Salvation Outside the Church? Tracing the History of the Catholic Response* (New York: Paulist Press, 1992), 158–59.
3. *SC* 53.

for others, or about the powerful presence of Christ the high
priest with whom the "priestly people" associate themselves
above all through celebrating the Eucharist. Apropos of this
final point, some years later Sullivan wrote: "The mediation of
the Church in the salvation of those it does not reach can be
seen in the fact that the Church offers the Eucharistic sacrifice
for the salvation of the whole world."[4] Here he came close to
naming the priestly intercession of the risen Christ and believers participating in it, but did not in fact make the connection.

Jacques Dupuis

Writing a few years later, Jacques Dupuis paid considerable
attention to Sullivan's book (*Salvation Outside the Church?*) and
also examined what the church's prayer for "others" involves.
This prayer exercises "moral" and "final" causality but not "efficient" causality. The church is an effective instrument of salvation for her own members, and mediates salvation to them by
proclaiming the Word of God and providing them with the
sacraments. But while the church intercedes for "the others,"
especially in the Eucharistic celebration, this prayer for "others" does not belong to the efficient but rather to the moral
order. Finality also comes into play, inasmuch as "the others"
are oriented toward the church.[5]

When presenting the church's intercessory prayer for
others, Dupuis, like Sullivan, cited the liturgy.[6] But, again like

---

4. F. A. Sullivan, "Introduction and Ecclesiological Issues," in S. J.
Pope and C. Hefling (eds.), *Sic et Non: Encountering Dominus Iesus* (Maryknoll, NY: Orbis Books, 2002), 47–56, at 50–51.

5. J. Dupuis, *Toward a Christian Theology of Religious Pluralism* (Maryknoll, NY: Orbis Books, 1997), 349–52. Dupuis repeated this view, often
in the same words, in *Christianity and the Religions: From Confrontation to
Dialogue* (Maryknoll, NY: Orbis Books, 2002), 210–13.

6. Dupuis quoted words from the Third Eucharistic Prayer ("Lord,
may this sacrifice, which has made our peace with you, advance the salvation of all the world") in both *Toward a Christian Theology* (350 n. 6) and
Christianity and the Religions (210–11).

Sullivan, he made no appeal to Vatican II's restoration of the
Prayer of the Faithful nor to the classic instruction the council quoted from 1 Timothy about prayer being made for all
human beings without exception: "I urge that supplications,
prayers, intercessions, and thanksgiving be made for everyone" (1 Tim. 2:1). In a later document, the Declaration on Religious Liberty, the council quoted this same verse when urging
all Catholics to pray for "the others" (*DH* 14), albeit without
relating the verse to the liturgy.[7] This verse from 1 Timothy
enjoys a certain importance in the NT and in the teaching of
Vatican II about "the others," but remained neglected by both
Sullivan and Dupuis.

Dupuis never introduced love as the driving force behind
any intercession for "the others." Nor did he observe how, at
the celebration of the Eucharist, the crucified and risen Christ
continues to practice his priestly ministry as mediator between
God and the whole of humankind. What of the "final" and
"moral" causality that Dupuis detects as being at work?[8]

First, "others" can be helped toward the church through the
graces they receive when Christians pray for them. The hoped-
for *finis* or goal orients them toward becoming members of
the church. The prayers of Christians for "the others" aim at
their *preparatio evangelica*, or their being teleologically directed
toward the future end of accepting the gospel and entering the
church through faith and baptism.

---

7. On 1 Timothy 2:1, see L. T. Johnson, *The First and Second Letters to
Timothy* (New York: Doubleday, 2000), 188–89, 194–95; and J. D. Quinn
and W. C. Wacker, *The First and Second Letters to Timothy* (Grand Rapids,
MI: Eerdmans, 2000), 159–63, 171–75. Quinn and Wacker suggest that
1 Timothy 2:1 "implies a gathering of believers, a liturgical setting, as
well as a continual, repeated activity" (at 172).

8. Scholastic theology, which, at least in passing, Dupuis borrowed,
appropriated Aristotle's classification of causes, in which the final cause
denoted the causality exercised by the goal or *telos* of some action. See
Benedict M. Ashley, "Final Causality," in *New Catholic Encyclopedia*, 2nd
ed. (Detroit: Gale, 2003), 5:723–27.

Like the Second Vatican Council, Dupuis recalled the (teleo-logical) theme of *preparatio evangelica*,[9] but he did so with ref-erence to other religions proving to be a preparation for the gospel.[10] He did not think of the church's intercession for "the others" as contributing to their being moved to the future goal of receiving the gospel. Yet, if these prayers of intercession have the purpose of orienting them toward the church, they belong, albeit mysteriously, to their *preparatio evangelica*. Unquestion-ably, what this preparation involves always goes beyond the church's intercessory prayer. Nevertheless, to explain this prayer for "the others" in the light of final causality necessarily involves recognizing a particular contribution to their *prepara-tio evangelica* coming from the prayers of Christians.

Second, Dupuis borrowed "the terminology of Scholastic theology" to argue that "where the church's intercession is con-cerned," the causality at work "seems to be of the moral rather than the efficient order.[11] Setting the classifications "moral" and "efficient" over and against each other did not, however, correspond to what Scholastic theology normally proposes. Alan Wolter, for instance, brings "moral causes" directly into his discussion of efficient causality and states that the "distinc-tion between moral and physical causes reflects" an extension of the notion of efficient causality as regards free agents. A physical cause produces an effect by its own direct action, either immediately or by way of some instrument. . . . A moral cause, however, usually refers to a person who by appeal, threat, or the like, induces a second person to act."[12] Thus "moral" causality turns out to be a particular form of efficient causality, which

---

9. On this theme in Vatican II documents, see G. O'Collins, *The Sec-ond Vatican Council on Other Religions* (Oxford: Oxford University Press, 2013), 77–79, 115–16.

10. Dupuis, *Toward a Christian Theology*, 131, 134, 162–64; Dupuis, *Christianity and the Religions*, 46, 155.

11. Dupuis, *Christianity and the Religions*, 211; here Dupuis repeated what he had already written in *Toward a Christian Theology*, 350.

12. A. B. Wolter, "Efficient Causality," in *New Catholic Encyclopedia*, 5:98–102, at 99.

differs from physical causality by producing its effect through personal influence rather than through physical action.

Dupuis was concerned to distinguish between (a) the instrumental causality exercised by the church for the benefit of her members through, for instance, the "instrumentality" of the sacraments, and (b) what the church does for "the others" through intercessory prayer. Yet attributing *moral* causality to the church's intercession leaves us within the area of efficient causality, even if this is a form of efficient causality exercised through personal influence rather than through the physical actions of the sacramental order.

In the light of these clarifications, Dupuis's position faces various questions: How should he have interpreted in detail the moral causality exercised by the church's intercessory prayer? Does the church when engaged in that prayer enjoy "personal influence" over the ways in which God will act toward "the others"? Could such a prayer even be a necessary condition for God helping "the others" and doing for them things that would not otherwise be done for them? What would happen to "the others," if we, the church as a whole, did not pray for them, as enjoined by 1 Timothy and Vatican II? These questions belong to a broader challenge. What is the impact of petitionary and intercessory prayer? Should we conceive of it as even changing what God is going to do for any person or group of persons? We return to these questions below.

Gavin D'Costa

In a 2009 book, Gavin D'Costa discussed differences between Sullivan and Dupuis.[13] After recalling that "the Eucharist is the eternal sacrifice of God's self-giving love," he considered the bidding prayers for Good Friday, both those in use before Vatican II and the revised version published after the council. In either form, these prayers that "instrumentally bring about a reality" have "an

---

13. G. D'Costa, *Christianity and World Religions: Disputed Questions in the Theology of Religions* (Malden, MA: Wiley-Blackwell, 2009), 180–86.

efficacious power because they are the prayers of the church." In similar words, he stated: "These prayers bring about an instrumental relation of efficacy to the unevangelized non-Christians."[14] Unlike Sullivan and Dupuis, D'Costa recognized how the church's bidding prayers prove relevant to the issue of its mediatory role for "the others." Yet he limited himself to the Good Friday liturgy, and, like Sullivan and Dupuis, failed to note the significance of (a) the Prayer of the Faithful reintroduced by the Second Vatican Council and of (b) the NT text to which it appealed (1 Tim. 2:1).

Moreover, if D'Costa wanted to borrow the terminology of causality from Scholastic theology, he needed to respect the traditional distinction between physical and moral causes quoted above from Wolter. A physical efficient cause, such as the sacrament of baptism, produces its effect instrumentally or as an instrument used by the principal cause or minister, the invisible but truly present risen Christ acting through his Holy Spirit. The prayers of the community are, to be sure, a particular form of efficient causality, but they differ from physical causes, such as baptism. As a moral cause, they produce their effect through personal appeal or influence rather than through physical action. They enjoy a causal role, but it is not an instrumental one, if we wish to apply the classifications of Scholastic theology.

Like Sullivan and Dupuis, D'Costa remained silent about the love that motivates the church's intercession for "the others." As we noted above, he did call the Eucharist "the eternal sacrifice of God's self-giving love." He also referred in passing to the "love and mercy of God."[15] But in examining the role of intercessory prayer for "others," we are concerned with the church's love for them, albeit a love inspired by divine action. Like Dupuis, D'Costa never mentioned the priestly quality of the people who participate in the Eucharist and lovingly pray

---

14. Ibid., 183, 185–86.

15. Ibid., 183, 185. Obviously what the Eucharist presents is not precisely "the eternal sacrifice of God's self-giving love," but the eternal sacrifice of the incarnate Son of God's self-giving love.

for "the others." Like Sullivan and Dupuis, D'Costa also failed to invoke the presence and action at the Eucharist of Christ the high priest.

Intercessory Prayer for "the Others"

An evaluation of what Sullivan, Dupuis, and D'Costa proposed and failed to propose can open the way for reflection on the church's intercession both for those who follow other living faiths and for those who profess no religious faith at all. Here intercessory prayer or asking on behalf of others should be distinguished from petitionary prayer or asking for ourselves. I say "distinguished," since a sharp separation does not seem in order. Both intercession and petition take us into the mysterious interaction between the divine will and the will of human beings, as well as leaving us to grapple with such problems as that of unanswered prayer and with the question: if the all-knowing, all-powerful, and perfectly good God already knows our needs and those of others, what is the point of either interceding for them or of petitioning for ourselves? The teaching of the NT (notably the Lord's Prayer) enjoins intercession for others and petitions for ourselves. But how can we understand and justify such interceding and petitioning?

Here the Christology of religions can be enriched by centuries of Christian reflection on prayer. From Origen and Augustine, through Thomas Aquinas, and down to the present day, the insights of theologians and philosophers about prayer throw light on what happens when Christians intercede for "the others."[16] Before introducing seven of their contributions,

---

16. See, e.g., P. R. Baelz, *Does God Answer Prayer?* (London: Darton, Longman & Todd, 1962); D. Basinger, "Why Petition an Omnipotent, Omniscient, and Wholly Good God?," *Religious Studies* 19 (1983): 25–41; V. Brümmer, *What Are We Doing When We Pray? On Prayer and the Nature of Faith*, 2nd ed. (Aldershot, UK: Ashgate, 2008); A. Cocksworth, *Karl Barth on Prayer* (London: T. & T. Clark, 2015); R. J. Foster, *Prayer: Finding the Heart's True Home* (San Francisco: HarperSan Francisco, 1992), 179–201; M. J. Murray, "Does God Respond to Petitionary Prayer?," in

let me make two preliminary observations about the great Intercessor and his disciples.

The risen Christ continues his high-priestly ministry of intercession for all the world (Rom. 8:34; Heb. 7:25). This intercession asks for mercy and forgiveness, as well as being perhaps a plea for deliverance from hostile powers.[17] However exegetes precisely explicate what Romans and Hebrews say about this priestly intercession: that it brings us close to what God continues to desire and do for Christians *and others alike.*

As regards the disciples of Jesus, according to the Fourth Gospel, they should pray to God in his name: "The Father will give you whatever you ask him in my name" (John 15:16). The theme recurs in the following chapter: "If you ask anything of the Father in my name, he will give it to you. Until now you have not asked for anything in my name. Ask, and you will receive, so that your joy may be complete" (John 16:23–24). This unqualified promise obviously leaves us with the challenge of seemingly unanswered prayers. What should Christians think of situations when they have prayed in the name of Jesus for themselves (petition) or for others (intercession) and not "received"? We will return below to the "efficacy" of the prayer of intercession. Here I wish to underline only that Christian intercession takes place "in the name of Jesus," the great Intercessor.

After these two preliminary observations we come to the issue of prayer "for others." What should a Christology of reli-

---

M. L. Petersen and R. J. VanArragon (eds.), *Contemporary Debates in the Philosophy of Religion* (Oxford: Blackwell, 2004), 242–55; M. J. Murray and K. Meyers, "Ask and It Will Be Given to You," *Religious Studies* 30 (1994): 311–30; M. Nedoncelle, *The Nature and Use of Prayer* (London: Burns & Oates, 1964); E. Stump, "Petitionary Prayer," in E. Stump and M. J. Murray (eds.), *Philosophy of Religion: The Big Questions* (Malden, MA: Blackwell, 1999), 353–66.

17. See J. A. Fitzmyer, *Romans: A New Translation with Introduction and Commentary* (New York: Doubleday, 1993), 533; C. R. Koester, *Hebrews: A New Translation with Introduction and Commentary* (New York: Doubleday, 2001), 366.

gions take on from the insights of philosophers and theologians who have wrestled with the nature of intercessory prayer "for others," and so promise to illuminate the brief teaching of the NT and the Second Vatican Council?

(1) "Intercession is a way of loving others."[18] This statement from Richard Foster should be uncontroversial. Admittedly, when 1 Timothy 2:1 and Vatican II (*SC* 53 and *DH* 14) urge that intercession be made for all human beings or for "the evangelization of the world" (*LG* 38; see 40), these texts do not appeal explicitly to the motivation of love. Yet, whether they consciously articulate their reasons or not, Christians show that they care deeply about "the others" and their future destiny when they pray for them and their salvation. Below we will come back to the function of love in all such intercession.

(2) "Intercessory prayer is *priestly* ministry."[19] Once again this observation should not be controversial. The baptized share in the responsibility of Christ's triple office; they are all priests, prophets/teachers, and kings/shepherds. In particular, they express their priestly identity by joining themselves —supremely, in the celebration of the Eucharist—to the self-offering of Christ and his intercession for human beings. As Sullivan rightly observed, it is in the Eucharistic setting that the "priestly people" exercise "this mediating role" for "the salvation of the whole world." This theme will be followed up below.

(3) Eleonore Stump describes the prayer of petition as "a request freely made to God for something *specific* believed to be good for those praying."[20] She uses to advantage the case of Monica praying for something specific, the conversion of her son Augustine.[21] (This is also a striking example of prayer being motivated by love—a theme that lay beyond the explicit

---

18. Foster, *Prayer*, 191.
19. Ibid.; emphasis mine.
20. Stump, "Petitionary Prayer," 353; emphasis mine.
21. Ibid., 361–63.

scope of Stump's article.) But does petition and, for that matter, intercession necessarily involve a request being made "for
something specific"? This may or may not be the case.

It makes perfectly good sense to speak, for example, of
someone praying for the general, spiritual well-being of his or
her country. The classic NT passage supporting the practice
of intercession mixes the general with some specifics (in particular, a request for tolerant policies on the part of worldly
authorities): "I urge that supplications, prayers, intercessions
and thanksgiving be made for everyone, [and, specifically,] for
kings and all who are in high positions, so that we [Christians]
may lead a quiet and peaceful life" (1 Tim. 2:1–2). When restor-
ing the Prayer of the Faithful, Vatican II's Constitution on the
Sacred Liturgy understood such intercession in general terms.
Even when a particular group ("those who lead us politically")
is mentioned, the council did not prescribe any specifics but
simply mandated: "Intercessions are to be made for the holy
church, for those who lead us politically, for those weighed
down by various needs, for all human beings, and for the salvation of the whole world" (*SC* 53).

In the case of the Lord's Prayer (Matt. 6:9–13), the opening
three "you" petitions that concern all humanity, which could
equally well or even better be called "intercessions," remain
very general: "May your name be made holy; may your kingdom come; may your will be done on earth as in heaven." The
first two of the four "we" requests exhibit a certain specificity:
"Give us today our daily bread; and forgive us our debts, as we
also have forgiven our debtors." But the final two "we" requests
remain rather general: "Do not bring us to the time of trial, but
rescue us from the evil one."[22]

(4) Since intercession exercises its own kind of *efficient causality* (see above), what changes does God, who has prompted

---

22. On the Lord's Prayer, see J. P. Meier, *A Marginal Jew: Rethinking the Historical Jesus* (New York: Doubleday, 1994), 2:291–302, 353–60,
363–4; G. O'Collins, *The Lord's Prayer* (London: Darton, Longman &
Todd, 2006).

such prayer, bring about "in response" to it? To begin with, making intercession for others and, in particular, for those who do not share Christian faith, signals some change (initiated and carried through by God) in those who join in such intercessions. Failure to pray for "the others" involves a failure on the part of Christians to be changed and made holy in the way God wants. Putting matters positively, we can argue that the prayer of intercession for "the others" will prove unfailingly efficacious in changing those who pray, even when—and this seems to be normally the case—they cannot identify any precise changes in those "others" that such prayer helped to effect. Interceding for "the others" has its necessary impact on those who intercede, through fostering their caring attitudes and shaping their loving selves.[23]

(5) Can we say, however, that, without those prayers, God will not help "the others" and bring about their salvation? God "desires everyone to be saved" (1 Tim. 2:4). But will God effect their salvation if Catholics and other Christians fail to intercede "for all human beings and for the salvation of the entire world" (*SC* 53)? Here we run up against what Paul calls the "unsearchable judgments" and "inscrutable ways" of God (Rom. 11:33).

As Stump remarks, "we do not know which states of affairs are divinely determined to occur regardless of prayer." And yet, for all we know, any given case of change for the better in others may be "one in which God would not have brought about the desired state of affairs" without the church interceding for it.[24] The prayer of Christians promotes the well-being of others, or at least their final well-being—so 1 Timothy seems to imply. But when and for which group of "others" does the church's prayer bring about this desired state of affairs (see point 7 below)?

---

23. In *What Are We Doing When We Pray?*, Brümmer quotes Kierkegaard ("Prayer changes the one who offers it"), Aquinas, Augustine, and others to establish the impact of prayer on those who pray (26–27).

24. Stump, "Petitionary Prayer," 357.

(6) When reflecting on the mystery of the divine providence for "the others," most Christians probably want to avoid two extremes. One extreme holds that God will never bestow needed blessings on "the others" unless the church intercedes for them. In other words, Christian intercession is necessary if they are to be saved. The other extreme holds that God would always bestow the blessings anyway, even without being asked. Everything is divinely predetermined, with the freely made prayer of Christians exercising no influence whatsoever on what happens to "the others."

Let me suggest a middle ground. Somehow God works or also works through the mediation of our intercessory prayer rather than simply bringing about everything on his own. God wants to associate the baptized with the divine work of caring for all "the others." Imitating the divine benevolence that extends to all people, the disciples of Jesus are to "love and pray" for everyone (Matt. 5:44–45). Apropos of such genuine love for one's neighbor, Karl Rahner remarked that God is always "the ground" and "mysterious partner" of such love.[25] Since this is true in general, it must hold all the more true at the Eucharist, when the baptized join their prayers for "the others" to the efficacious prayers of Christ the high priest, who lives forever interceding for all human beings. Christ is the cause, "ground," and "partner" of such prayer.

Here the setting for the Prayer of the Faithful proves highly significant. The First Letter of Timothy did not, or at least did not explicitly, propose the setting of the Eucharist when enjoining that "intercessions" be made "for everyone" (1 Tim. 2:1). But the Second Vatican Council, when retrieving this practice, stipulated expressly the celebration of the Eucharist as the context in which the prayer for all human beings should be practiced. This prayer of intercession, by belonging to the "liturgical celebration," becomes "a work (opus) of Christ the

---

25. K. Rahner, *Foundations of Christian Faith: An Introduction to the Idea of Christianity* (New York: Seabury Press, 1978), 309.

Priest and of his Body, which is the church." The Constitution on the Sacred Liturgy then adds confidently that "no action of the church," other than the liturgical celebration, "equals its efficacy (*efficacitatem*)" (*SC* 7). Hence, inasmuch as the liturgical intercessions "for the others" relate so closely to the priestly ministry of Christ himself, we should expect a generous divine response. It would be strange if this were not the case. Through baptism the faithful already share in the priestly ministry of Christ. They exercise this priestly ministry in a preeminent way when they join with him even more closely in celebrating the Eucharist and praying for the salvation of the whole world.

(7) This is not to say that it will be easy to identify in particular cases the impact of the church's intercession for "the others." Many other forces, both divine and human, can be at work in the changing situation of any specific group of "others." Let us consider one example. In 1884 Pope Leo XIII introduced the so-called Leonine Prayers for recitation immediately after Mass; they remained in general usage until 1964. After 1929, Pius XI prescribed that these prayers be said for the people of Russia, so that they might have the "tranquility and freedom to profess the faith."[26] Were these prayers eventually answered through the events of 1989 and its aftermath that signaled the end of European Communism? We might be cautious about proposing what has counted as an answer to the Leonine Prayers.

Nevertheless, while being properly tentative about identifying the precise efficacy of these prayers and other particular intercessions, we should never discount the efficacy of praying for "the others," especially in the context of liturgical celebrations. Prayer can and does affect the ways God lovingly influences "others," even if we need to be cautious about deciding when, how, and for whom this happens.

---

26. See F. A. Brunner, "Leonine Prayers," in *New Catholic Encyclopedia*, 8:500.

Love Inspires Intercession

We saw above how the limited discussion of Christian intercessory prayer for "the others" has failed to reflect on love and its
impact. Yet we recalled how in the Sermon on the Mount Jesus
associated prayer for "others" with love. How will love inspire
prayer? What could its relevance, "causal" or otherwise, be to
intercession for "the others"? Over many centuries, Christian
theology, philosophy, biblical studies, and other disciplines
have offered a wealth of ideas about love.[27] Let me retrieve
three themes that illuminate the nature and power of praying
for "others."

First, love is inherently relational and committed to others,
or, as many express matters nowadays, altruistic. This means
that even before they move to help others and do so even at
considerable cost to themselves, those who love others accept,
approve, wonder at, and rejoice in these others, whether they
are Buddhists, Confucians, Hindus, Muslims, Sikhs, or whatever. They sympathetically respond to and affirm these others
for what they are in themselves, particular and mysterious
manifestations of created reality and goodness.

Medieval thought called this initial characteristic of love the
"love of delight" (*amor complacentiae*). When the community
of the baptized joins with Christ in praying for "the others,"
like him it fundamentally approves of them for their unique
personal reality. Every one of these "others" enjoys intrinsic,
incomparably different value for God, the risen Christ, and the
Holy Spirit. Whether they are conscious of this or not, Christians who practice what 1 Timothy enjoins about praying for
the salvation of everyone share Christ's fundamental "love of
delight" in each and every human being.

---

27. For a bibliography on love, see G. O'Collins and D. Kendall, *The
Bible for Theology: Ten Principles for the Theological Use of Scriptures* (Mah-
wah, NJ: Paulist Press, 1997), 178–79; W. J. Jeanrond, *A Theology of Love*
(London: T. & T. Clark, 2010), 261–79; and T. J. Oord, *Defining Love: A
Philosophical, Scientific, and Theological Engagement* (Grand Rapids, MI:
Brazos, 2010), *passim*.

Second, such loving approval involves identifying with "the others," caring for them, taking responsibility for them, and making their interests our own. As the "love of benevolence" (*amor benevolentiae*), love reaches out to serve the interests of these "others," advances their welfare because we love them, and does so, in particular, by our self-giving.

The redemption of human beings involved nothing less than the self-gift of the Son of God in person and then the divine self-gift that was the sending of the Holy Spirit. In lovingly bestowing what is true, good, and beautiful, God came with the gift. All divine giving is self-giving, and so too is all authentic human giving. The "agapeic" activity that flows in spontaneous abundance from the divine goodness communicates nothing less than the divine reality.

The intercessory prayer of Christians for "the others" entails an active concern for them that, in fact, participates in the self-giving of the risen Christ and of the Holy Spirit. Truly, if mysteriously, the Son and the Spirit are present in all people and at work transforming their lives (Chap. 3 above). Thus, praying for "the others," whether Christians are conscious or not of what it involves, means nothing less than sharing in the universal, "benevolent" love of God expressed and active in the "missions" of the Son and the Holy Spirit. Such intercessory prayer lets the baptized enter into the effective divine love deployed for the ultimate welfare of all human beings. The baptized become participants in a universal divine activity of love.

A third characteristic of love seems to create difficulty if applied to the prayers of intercession for "the others." Without a *reciprocity* that brings a lasting, mutual *union* (*amor unionis*), love remains radically incomplete and merely a kind of unilateral generosity. Love by its very nature longs for community with "the others" and aims at establishing and maintaining a permanent relationship in mutual freedom.[28] Such reciprocity shapes Jesus' call to discipleship. John's Gospel associates love with the mutual relationship involved in following Jesus

---

28. O'Collins and Kendall, *The Bible for Theology*, 63–65.

through life and death (John 21:15–19). This reciprocal relationship lives itself out in a permanent loving union with him
and in the fellowship of the Christian community. Paul's letters
testify to the reciprocated presence of divine love at the heart
of the young churches. The apostle reaches for the image of
marriage when portraying the community's graced and loving
union with Christ (2 Cor. 11:2; see Eph. 5:25–32).

The prayer of intercession may bring the reciprocity and
fellowship that is longed for when groups of "others" come
to Christian faith and through baptism enter the church. But
it is obvious that, in the case of many millions, such prayer
may seemingly not be publicly answered and enjoy such a clear
outcome. Nevertheless, the hidden but efficacious presence of
Christ and the Holy Spirit in the life of every human being
brings its fruit.[29] Even without becoming aware of Christ and
his Spirit, human beings can act in ways that respond to the
divine promptings and reciprocate the redeeming love that
they mysteriously experience.

To sum up: love inspires the intercessory prayer through
which the faithful associate themselves with the saving love
exercised toward all human beings by the risen Christ and his
Spirit. They do this in a preeminent way when they celebrate
the Eucharist and participate in Christ the high priest's self-
offering on behalf of all people.

Here we should not forget the *epiclesis* (invocation) of the
Holy Spirit, which in the Eucharistic prayers asks that the Spirit
descend upon the gifts of the community and change them
into the body and blood of Christ, and do so for the spiritual
profit of those who receive the sacrament. The reform of the
liturgy after the Second Vatican Council inserted into the new
canons (composed for the Western church) an *epiclesis* before
the words of institution (praying that the gifts be changed) and
after those words (praying that the community be changed).
Invoking the Holy Spirit, the personal Love between Father

---

29. See O'Collins, *The Second Vatican Council on Other Religions*, 158–
66.

and Son, will change those who share in the Eucharist and will lovingly empower their prayers of intercession for "the others."

Participating in the Priesthood of Christ

As was pointed out above, the priesthood of Christ has been neglected by those engaged in the theology of religions and, in particular, by those reflecting on the efficacy of Christian intercession for "the others." That intercession is incorporated into the eternal ministry of Christ the high priest. Above all, at the Eucharist and through the power of the Holy Spirit, the crucified and risen Christ presents lovingly to the Father his self-offering on behalf of all people and draws into his self-offering the church's intercession for them.

A recent book by Garry Wills would undercut this picture by rejecting not only the validity of Christian priesthood but also the priestly identity of Jesus himself. To make his case, Wills argues that the Letter to the Hebrews went astray in recognizing the priesthood of Christ. "A polished writer" but "no profound thinker," the author of Hebrews produced "flimsy," "capricious," and even "fallacious" arguments when portraying Christ as "a priest forever according to the order of Melchizedek."[30]

One should take issue with Wills over various dubious claims: for instance, that among the books of the NT, Hebrews stands alone in recognizing Christ as priest. Without explicitly using the title, the Gospel of John implies that priesthood. In the Fourth Gospel's portrayal of Jesus, he embodies the significance of several major festivals—above all, the Passover. The feeding of the five thousand and the discourse that follows on the bread of life occur, as only John observes, at the time of the Passover (John 6:4). Andrew Lincoln writes: "As the true

---

30. G. Wills, *Why Priests? A Failed Tradition* (New York: Viking, 2013), 107–15, 156. Without showing historical sensitivity, Wills dismisses as "eccentric logic" (119, 120) what belonged to first-century, Jewish methods of biblical interpretation.

bread from heaven, Jesus fulfills what was signified not only by the manna of the exodus but also by the unleavened bread of the Passover, and Jesus' flesh and blood are now the food and drink of the true Passover meal."[31] Through his priestly self-gift, Jesus has replaced the Passover festival. This replacement motif in the Fourth Gospel expresses aspects of Jesus' identity and function as both priest and victim. It is deployed through such features as Jesus replacing the Temple and its cult (2:13–22) and his being "the lamb of God" (1:29, 36), whose death occurs at the hour when the Passover lambs are being slaughtered (19:14, 31).[32]

Wills maintains that the Last Supper was only "an eschatological meal like the other meals and feedings" in the Gospels; in the early church, he claims, there was no "re-enactment" of the Last Supper.[33] But the Gospels, Paul's letters, and 1 Timothy encourage us to take issue with both claims.

While the evangelists understood the earlier "feedings" to prefigure the Last Supper, they never pictured Jesus as saying on those occasions: "This is my body" and "this is my blood poured out for all." The Last Supper was "like" the previous meals, but was also unlike them and went beyond them. As a sacrificial meal, the Last Supper implied priestly activity on the part of Jesus. Through the words and gestures of the "institution narrative," Jesus offered a covenant sacrifice—a cultic, priestly act that he wanted to be continued in the community he had begun to gather.[34] We know from Paul that this sacrificial meal was "re-enacted" in the Christian communities, when they celebrated "the covenant" sealed with the blood of Christ (1 Cor. 11:23–26).[35]

---

31. A. T. Lincoln, *The Gospel According to John* (London: Continuum, 2005), 76–77.

32. On the priesthood of Christ in John's Gospel, see further G. O'Collins and M. K. Jones, *Jesus Our Priest: A Christian Approach to the Priesthood of Christ* (Oxford: Oxford University Press, 2010), 24–26.

33. Wills, *Why Priests?*, 17, 224.

34. O'Collins and Jones, *Jesus Our Priest*, 19–24.

35. Ibid., 28–30.

Paul, along with the early traditions he draws on, understands the death of Christ to be a sacrifice and does so with specific reference to the Day of Expiation (Rom. 3:24–26). Later this same letter anticipates Hebrews' vision of priesthood by referring to the heavenly intercession of the crucified and risen Christ (Rom. 8:34). Paul goes on to employ cultic language in picturing the "priestly" existence that Christians are empowered to live (Rom. 12:1). Wills remarks that Paul never calls himself a priest.[36] But Paul does call himself a "liturgist/minister" in the "priestly service" of the gospel, offering his evangelization of the Gentiles as a form of worship or sacrifice to God (Rom. 15:15–16).[37]

The First Letter of Timothy famously states that "there is one mediator between God and humankind, Christ Jesus" (1 Tim. 2:5). Hebrews also calls Christ "mediator," and does so three times when it presents his priestly work as that of "the mediator of the new/better covenant" (Heb. 8:6; 9:15; 12:24). Wills wants to undercut priestly implications by proposing to translate *mesitēs* as "guarantor."[38] But the word is translated uniformly as "mediator" by current versions of the NT (e.g. the New American Bible, the New International Version, the New Jerusalem Bible, the New Revised Standard Version, and the Revised English Bible) as well as by such standard lexicons as the *Greek-English Lexicon of the New Testament and Other Early Christian Literature* (BDAG).[39]

Wills rightly castigates the sins of clericalism that have victimized many innocent people and seriously harmed the life of the church. But such a reformist agenda should not lead to the

---

36. Wills, *Why Priests?*, 14.

37. About the priestly ministry of Christ in which his followers share, Paul has much to say, as do 1 Peter and Revelation; see O'Collins and Jones, *Jesus Our Priest*, 28–44. Wills ignores much of this testimony about Christians exercising a priestly ministry.

38. Wills, *Why Priests?*, 266.

39. F. W. Danker (ed.), *Greek-English Lexicon of the New Testament and Other Early Christian Literature*, 3rd ed. (Chicago: University of Chicago Press, 2000).

wholesale discrediting of the priesthood of Christ, in which the baptized and the ordained share. Wills has put his negative case at a time when many Catholics, now led by Pope Francis, have set themselves to regain and implement the full teaching of Vatican II. In *Sacrosanctum Concilium*, the council proposed a liturgical reform that went hand in hand with a renewed sense of Christ's priesthood: the liturgy "is rightly seen as an exercise of the priestly office of Jesus Christ." Every liturgical celebration is nothing less than "an action of Christ the priest and of his body, which is the church" (*SC* 7). Later, the same constitution vividly pictures Christ exercising his priestly ministry not only for and with members of the church who assemble for worship but also for and with the entire world. It states: "Jesus Christ, the high priest of the new and eternal covenant, when he assumed a human nature, introduced into this land of exile the hymn that in heaven is sung throughout the ages. He unites the whole community of humankind with himself and associates it with him in singing the divine canticle of praise" (*SC* 83). When recalling the liturgical constitution and quoting several passages from it, Wills avoids such references to Christ's role as high priest.[40] They would not suit his argument against Christ being a priest.

While Wills wants to demolish the notion of Christ's priesthood, a Christian theologian from the Reformed tradition, Graham Redding, has been concerned to focus the Eucharistic liturgy clearly on the mediatorial priesthood of Christ. He argues that unless Christ's priesthood is properly appreciated, the liturgy remains confused and impoverished. That priesthood must be expressed liturgically if the public prayer of the church is to function as it should—through conscious participation in the eternal offering Christ makes of himself (in the Spirit) to the Father. Where an authentic doctrine of Christ's priesthood is missing, worship can become more and more

---

40. Wills, *Why Priests?*, 60–65.

dependent on the talents and personality of the minister who leads the congregation in prayer.[41]

Redding attends to the life of the church at prayer—and especially to a theme wonderfully developed by the late Thomas Torrance: namely, the need for conscious participation in the eternal self-offering of the risen and ascended Christ.[42] But Christ continues to exercise his priesthood not only for the baptized who assemble for worship but also for the wider world. *Sacrosanctum Concilium* reminds us, as we have seen above, that he functions as high priest for all human beings, many of whom may never have heard his name (*SC* 83). Through their prayers of intercession, especially at the Eucharist, the faithful join with the risen Christ in lovingly exercising their priestly ministry for those who follow "other" faiths or none at all.

Conclusion

After taking up the views of Sullivan, Dupuis, and D'Costa on the church's intercession for "the others," this chapter set out to clarify the Scholastic terminology of "final" and "moral" causality introduced by Dupuis. It then moved (a) to illustrating how 1 Timothy and the Vatican II's liturgical constitution elucidate the church's intercession for "the others." Here a long tradition of theological-philosophical reflection on the efficacy of prayer must also be allowed to make its contribution and no longer remain ignored. When interpreting the power of intercession for "the others," one must also recognize how (b) it is inspired by love and embodies three major characteristics of love as approval, active benevolence, and a drive toward reciprocal unity. Here, as elsewhere, love should be understood as a genuinely efficient cause. Even if we can only guess at their

---

41. G. Redding, *Prayer and the Priesthood of Christ in the Reformed Tradition* (London: T. & T. Clark, 2003).

42. For details on Torrance, see O'Collins and Jones, *Jesus Our Priest*, 224–29.

effects in the unfolding history of the human race, prayers, inspired by love and embodying the power of love, enjoy their causal impact. The efficacy of prayer is drawn from the efficacy of love. By drawing the baptized into his activity of universal intercession, Christ makes them his instruments in a supreme work of love, the *opus redemptionis* being understood as an efficacious *opus amoris*. Finally, (c) such intercession, as just stated, brings the faithful to share in Christ's high-priestly activity for the whole world.

In these three ways, I aspire to enrich the discussion about other faiths, transforming it from a theology of religions to a Christology of religions. I do so at a time when, to borrow a phrase from Kevin Hart's latest collection of poetry,[43] so much of the talk about pluralism, inclusivism, exclusivism, particularism, and other "-isms" could remind us of "cupboards of useless clothes." Debates among theologians of religion seem to have reached a stalemate, and not least about the salvific power of "other" religions.[44] Some scholars have been calling for a moratorium, at least in some of the contested areas.[45]

Discussion could be happily moved forward by introducing themes that are significant but have so far been left out in the cold: the force of intercessory prayer for "the others," the power embodied in the love that motivates this prayer, and sharing in the universally relevant priesthood of Christ. Add also the themes developed in previous chapters: the universal presence of Christ and the Holy Spirit, and the theology of the cross. Do all these ideas make a fresh contribution to the theology of

---

43. K. Hart, *Wild Track* (Notre Dame, IN: University of Notre Dame Press, 2015), 34.

44. See my "Vatican II on 'Other' Ways of Salvation: A Valid Interpretation?," *Irish Theological Quarterly* 81 (2016): 152–70, where I suggest that the stalemate may be partly caused by a failure to update methods for interpreting texts—specifically, the documents of Vatican II.

45. See Catherine Cornille, "Soteriological Agnosticism and the Future of Catholic Theology of Interreligious Dialogue," in T. Merrigan and J. Friday (eds.), *The Past, Present, and Future of Theologies of Interreligious Dialogue* (Oxford: Oxford University Press, 2017), 201–15.

religions (better called the Christology of religions) and open up new insights that have not been previously developed? So far some of these five themes (for instance, the universal priesthood of Christ, exercised for the good of all human beings) have remained an untold story in the theology/Christology of religions.

We move next to develop in greater detail something initially developed in Chapter 2 above and which can also enrich the Christology of religions: the possibility of faith for "the others."

5

The Faith of the Suffering "Others"

Jacques Dupuis and many other scholars who have contributed to the theology of religions and a few, like Paul Griffiths, who write in the area of the philosophy of religion, have dedicated much attention to *salvation* for those who belong to other religions (or none at all). But they have paid less attention to the question of divine *revelation* reaching them. Since human faith forms the response to God's self-revelation, this (relative) neglect of revelation has *also* meant a similar (and often even greater) neglect of the question: In the light of the scriptures and, in particular, in the light of NT teaching, how might we understand and interpret the *faith* of those who follow other religions?

One might speculate about the reasons for highlighting salvation but neglecting divine revelation and the reciprocal human faith. Undoubtedly the ancient slogan "outside the church no salvation" (*extra ecclesiam nulla salus*), which continued to cast its long shadow for many centuries, has encouraged a one-sided attention to the issue of salvation for those who practice other faiths.[1] There was no parallel slogan "outside

---

1. See Bernard Sesboüé, *Hors de l'Église pas de salut: Histoire d'une formule et problèmes d'interpretation* (Paris: Desclée, 2004); Francis A. Sullivan, *Salvation Outside the Church?* (New York: Paulist Press, 1992).

the church no revelation" (*extra ecclesiam nulla revelatio*), which might have called for reflection on the divine self-revelation *and* responding human faith for "the others." We need to illustrate this imbalance before making any proposals about a biblical possibility for reflecting on the faith of those who follow other religions.

But before examining this imbalance, we should not ignore the setting of evil and suffering in which the question of faith arises. Trafficking in human beings, arms, and drugs continues to prove a terrible scourge for the world. By the end of 2016, savage local wars and persecutions have resulted in sixty million people becoming refugees, asylum seekers, or displaced persons, with millions of them experiencing a lack of sufficient food, decent housing, basic medical care, and educational possibilities. Reckless exploitation of fossil fuels and other natural resources, along with unchecked deforestation, have ravaged the earth and contributed to the spread of deserts, undernourishment, and straight starvation. The powerful people of rich nations find themselves beneficiaries of previously unheard of advantages built upon the sufferings of others. So many have not yet taken on board the prophetic words that Pope Francis repeats about "the globalization of indifference."

Victims of sexual abuse, domestic violence, and mass shootings, as well as legions of homeless and street people, constantly express the way of the cross (the *via crucis*) and the horror of Calvary. In such a context, for very many people life can become unbearable, and suffering can prompt a destructive breakdown. Yet there is also the possibility of a breakthrough, with faith working a personal and social transformation. By freely choosing to believe, sufferers experience the liberating impact of God's presence. It is at our peril, I would insist, that we ignore the setting of pain and evil in which faith can emerge for Christians and others alike. Below I will make this case by appealing to what the Letter to the Hebrews indicates about faith *and suffering*—specifically for those men and women who are not Christians.

Jacques Dupuis, Paul Griffiths, and Others

The lengthy index entries under "salvation" and "salvation history" in his final book reflect how Dupuis continued to privilege the question of salvation for the others.[2] Admittedly, he discussed in two sections, albeit briefly, the revelation that reaches them and their responding human faith.[3] He did so in the light of what he called "genuine religious experience" and "authentic prayer," understood as signs of such revelation taking place and evoking faith.

"Wherever there is a *genuine religious experience*," Dupuis wrote, "it is surely the God revealed in Jesus Christ who thus enters into the lives of men and women, in a hidden secret fashion." Authentic prayer on the part of human beings witnesses to the fact that their religious experience is "genuine," and that God has taken the initiative to reveal himself to them: "*Authentic prayer* is always a sign that God, in some secret and hidden way, has undertaken the initiative of a personal approach to human beings in self-revelation and has been welcomed by these human beings." Dupuis pressed on to specify this welcome as faith: "Those who entrust themselves to God in *faith* and charity are *saved*, however imperfect their conception of the God who has revealed himself to them." He added: "*Salvation* depends on the response made by sinful human beings in *faith* to a personal communication initiated by God."[4] The references to salvation indicate how it remained the predominant issue for Dupuis, even when he (very briefly) discussed divine self-revelation to "others" and their human response of faith.

Later and in passing, Dupuis remarked that "divine revelation" is "not to be considered monolithically, but as a diversified and complex reality."[5] The biblical record of revelation, with its

2. J. Dupuis, *Christianity and the Religions: From Confrontation to Dialogue* (Maryknoll, NY: Orbis Books, 2002), 273.

3. Ibid., 114–37, 230–31.

4. Ibid., 122; emphasis added.

5. Ibid., 135.

differing means and mediators along with its progressive character, emphatically supports this observation.[6] Dupuis might have added that, correspondingly, the response that human faith makes to revelation is also not to be considered monolithically but as a diversified and complex reality. There were and are different ways of responding with faith to diversified forms of revelation and living a "faithful" lifestyle. The entry on "faith" in the *Anchor Bible Dictionary* amply exemplifies this variety. For instance, in the Letter to the Hebrews *"pistis,"* in contrast to Paul and John, is "not used in connection with the Christological content, but it marks the way which those who belong to Christ, as Son and High Priest, must follow." It "means above all 'perseverance,' the holding fast to a promised hope."[7] As we shall see, the account of faith offered by Hebrews can also be applied to those who persevere in holding fast to a promised hope without consciously belonging to Christ.

In *Problems of Religious Diversity*, Paul Griffiths presents "salvation" (but neither revelation nor faith) in an opening, two-page account of key terms,[8] and, as the index illustrates, has more to say about salvation than about revelation and faith.[9] The book ends with a chapter on "The Question of Salvation."[10] Salvation is a key term for him, but not revelation or faith.

When discussing Karl Barth's criticism of religion, Griffiths speaks in passing of "responding to the living God with faith,"[11]

---

6. For varying features of revelation, see G. O'Collins, *Rethinking Fundamental Theology: Toward a New Fundamental Theology* (Oxford: Oxford University Press, 2012), 56–165.

7. Joseph P. Healey and Dieter Lührmann, "Faith," in *ABD*, 2:744–58, at 755. This entry discusses six forms of "faith" to be found in the NT: in Paul, the Deutero-Paulines, the Synoptic Gospels, the Johannine tradition, Hebrews, and James. See also Rudolf Bultmann et al., *"Pisteuō, pistis,"* etc., in *Theological Dictionary of the New Testament*, ed. Gerhard Kittel (Grand Rapids, MI: Eerdmans, 1968), 6:174–228.

8. P. J. Griffiths, *Problems of Religious Diversity* (Malden, MA: Blackwell, 2001), xv.

9. Ibid., 173, 175.

10. Ibid., 138–69.

11. Ibid., 152.

and so draws attention to the subjective, personal commitment of faith (what many call the *fides qua*). But generally he presents faith as *fides quae*, or the assent to truths or "claims" revealed by God and so to be held *de fide*. He writes of "claims revealed by God," to which it is "a matter of faith" to assent.[12] Hence he can describe faith as "faith in facts" (rather than faith in the living God who has personally approached human beings). For Christians this "faith in facts" means, for instance, accepting that Jesus Christ is the second person of the triune God.[13] The revelation that elicits such faith in facts, rather than being understood *primarily* as God's personal self-manifestation, amounts to what many call a propositional affair, or revelation understood to be the disclosure of otherwise inaccessible truths that are to be accepted, "preserved, and transmitted."[14]

A propositional account of faith inevitably involves a propositional view of revelation, and vice versa, with faith being primarily an assent to truths now revealed by God.[15] For this scheme, even if Griffiths may want to leave things open for those of other religions (whom he calls "religious aliens"), by privileging the content of faith (the *fides quae*) he makes it more difficult for Christians to acknowledge any faith exercised by these others. However, as we shall see, the Letter to the Hebrews offers a different vision of faith. It links a limited content (*fides quae*) to a steadfast loyalty (*fides qua*) that can be seen to characterize the faith not only of Christian believers but also of those who profess other religions.

We could continue to sample recent writing in the theology of religion and see how its exponents prefer to reflect on salvation for the followers of other religions and hence fail to treat

---

12. Ibid., 95.
13. Ibid., 133.
14. Ibid. 62, 63.
15. But, as the late Cardinal Avery Dulles wrote in reliance on Thomas Aquinas, "faith is not primarily propositional." See A. Dulles, "Faith and Unbelief," in Karl-Josef Becker and Ilaria Morali (eds.), *Catholic Engagement with World Religions: A Comprehensive Study* (Maryknoll, NY: Orbis Books, 2010), 303–14, at 313.

sufficiently the divine self-revelation or at least the human faith that this revelation initiates. S. Mark Heim entitled his 1995 book *Salvations: Truth and Difference in Religion*, and paid much more attention to matters of salvation than to revelation.[16] A 605-page book, edited by Karl Josef (later Cardinal) Becker and Ilaria Morali, repeatedly examines issues of human salvation and divine revelation, expounds the faith of Christians, but has little to say about the possibility of faith for others.[17]

Ad Gentes on Revelation and Faith

The Second Vatican Council's Decree on the Church's Missionary Activity (*Ad Gentes*) has, in three ways, significant things to say about the presence of revelation (with responding human faith) and salvation that characterizes or can characterize the religious situation of those who have not or who have not yet accepted faith in Christ. First, it picks up the Johannine terminology of "truth and grace" (John 1:14, 17) to recognize how Christ, "the author" of these elements, is already present among "the nations" even before they hear the word of Christian preaching. As giver of the gifts of revelation ("truth") and salvation ("grace"), he has already come to the nonevangelized, albeit mysteriously with his gifts (*AG* 9). The implication is clear: to the extent that these "others" respond positively to this prior offer of truth (or revelation), they respond with faith.

Second, by its preaching and sacraments the church aims to open up for all human beings the way "to participate *fully* in the mystery of Christ" (*AG* 5; emphasis mine). Once again, an important implication is clear: even before people respond with faith to the revelatory preaching of the church and accept salvation through baptism and the other sacraments, they can

---

16. S. M. Heim, *Salvations: Truth and Difference in Religion* (Maryknoll, NY: Orbis Books, 1995).

17. Becker and Morali, *Catholic Engagement with World Religions*, 86–88, 91–142, 368–79, 408–12, 447–58 (on salvation); 113–14, 117–19, 230–52, 360–68, 501–2 (on revelation); 153–206 (on the faith of Christians); 138, 303 (on the possible faith of non-Christians).

participate, albeit not yet fully, in the revealing and saving mystery of Christ.[18]

Third, *Ad Gentes* follows St. Irenaeus to state that the Son, "present in creation," "reveals" (*revelat*) the Father universally (*AG* 3). The decree then goes on to complete the picture by referring to the faith prompted, as it always must be, by revelation. Those human beings who are "inculpably ignorant of the gospel" can be "led to faith (*fides*), without which it is impossible to please" God (*AG* 7; see Heb. 11:6).[19]

Apropos of this possibility of being led to faith, the Congregation for the Doctrine of the Faith's declaration of 2000, *Dominus Iesus* ("the Lord Jesus"), contrasted the "theological faith" (*fides theologalis*) of Christians with the "belief" (*credulitas*) of those who follow other religions.[20] The former means "the acceptance in grace of revealed truth," whereas the latter is "the sum of experience and thought that constitutes the human treasury of wisdom and religious aspiration, which man in his search for truth has conceived and acted upon in his

---

18. This prior, less-than-full participation takes nothing away from the church's "need to evangelize" (*AG* 7); indeed it makes missionary activity as urgent as ever, if people are going to reach full faith and share in the sacraments of salvation.

19. For a fuller treatment of *AG* on the divine revelation that can universally trigger human faith, see G. O'Collins, *The Second Vatican Council on Other Religions* (Oxford: Oxford University Press, 2013), 109–27. The council fathers debated the final draft of *AG* and then an emended version of it on October 7–11, 1965, and November 10–11, 1965, respectively; see the *Acta* for details. On Yves Congar's central role in creating and emending *AG*, especially its first chapter, see O'Collins, *The Second Vatican Council on Other Religions*, 109–11.

20. Like most commentators on the Second Vatican Council, the Congregation for the Doctrine of the Faith failed to notice the language of universal "revelation" already used in *AG* 3 before the decree went on to speak of the corresponding universal possibility of faith. One should also add that Vatican II in its sixteen documents never introduced the terms *fides theologalis* and *credulitas*. Only a generous translation renders the latter term as "belief"; the original Latin would be more accurately rendered as "credulity" or "gullibility."

relationship to God." In short, it is "religious experience still in search of the absolute truth and still lacking assent to God who reveals himself" (*DI* 7).

This teaching forgot, however, that God is already present in any religious search (St. Anselm, *Proslogion* 1); human beings seek God because God has first "found" them. As St. Irenaeus of Lyons wrote in the second century, "No one can know God unless God teaches [him or her]: that is to say, without God, God cannot be known" (*Deum scire nemo potest, nisi Deo docente: hoc est, sine Deo non cognosci Deum*; *Adversus Haereses*, 4.6.4). What *Dominus Iesus* claimed also appeared incompatible with *Ad Gentes* 7, which took seriously Hebrews 11:6 ("without faith it is impossible to please God") and acknowledged that God can lead to faith those who, through no fault of their own, do not know the gospel and may be followers of major world religions, members of ethnic religions, and so forth. The divine self-revelation and responding human faith are genuine possibilities for all these "others."[21]

Here the Second Vatican Council points us toward the Letter of the Hebrews. It takes up, and applies to the nonevangelized, one verse of Hebrews (11:6). Unquestionably, the author of Hebrews wrote for Christians, and, even when expounding

---

21. See further O'Collins, *The Second Vatican Council on Other Religions*, 117–19. On texts (e.g. Hebrews) being relatively independent from their original authors (and readers), see Hans-Georg Gadamer, *Truth and Method*, 2nd ed. (New York: Crossroad, 1989). He states a universally valid principle: "Not just occasionally, but always, the meaning of a text goes beyond its author." When repeating this point, Gadamer adds that texts also become independent from their original addressees: "The horizon of understanding cannot be limited either by what the writer [e.g. the anonymous author of Hebrews] originally had in mind or by the horizon of the person to whom the text was originally addressed [e.g. the Christians to whom Hebrews was sent]" (296, 395). On the interpretive theory of Gadamer and the similar proposals of Paul Ricoeur, see the Pontifical Biblical Commission, *The Interpretation of the Bible in the Church* (Rome: Libreria Editrice Vaticana, 1993), 74–75. See also Ingolf U. Dalferth and Marlene A. Block (eds.), *Hermeneutics and the Philosophy of Religion: The Legacy of Paul Ricoeur* (Tübingen: Mohr Siebeck, 2015).

a general principle ("without faith it is impossible to please God"), did not have in mind the nonevangelized or those not yet evangelized. Nevertheless, we are justified in following Vatican II and acknowledging the relevance of Hebrews to those never expressly envisaged by its author. This text can always communicate more than its author ever consciously intended.[22] What if we follow the council's lead and read Hebrews 11 closely for what it has to offer? Elsewhere I have done this more briefly but without offering a full treatment and not yet adverting to the setting of suffering.[23]

Hebrews on Faith

The Faith of Christians

Coming from a priestly milieu, Hebrews calls on Christian leaders to speak the Word of God, give a shining example in living their Christian faith, and watch over those whose faith may be eroded by strange teachings (11:7, 15). The author of Hebrews urges the community to obey their leaders, who themselves are accountable to God (13:17). As a "word of encouragement" (13:22), the letter is to be presented orally to a community of Christians gathered for worship.[24]

---

22. For the interpretation of biblical and other texts, see O'Collins, *Rethinking Fundamental Theology*, 254–61, and O'Collins, "Vatican II on 'Other' Ways of Salvation: A Valid Interpretation?," *Irish Theological Quarterly* 81 (2016): 152–70.

23. O'Collins, *Rethinking Fundamental Theology*, 61–65, 317–18; and O'Collins, *Salvation for All: God's Other Peoples* (Oxford: Oxford University Press, 2008), 252–59.

24. On Hebrews and faith in Hebrews, see Harold W. Attridge, *The Epistle to the Hebrews* (Philadelphia: Fortress Press, 1989); Richard J. Bauckham (ed.), *The Epistle to the Hebrews and Christian Theology* (Grand Rapids, MI: Eerdmans, 2009); Gerhard Dautzenberg, "Der Glaube in Hebräerbrief," *Biblische Zeitschrift* 17 (1973): 161–77; Erich Grässer, *Der Glaube im Hebräerbrief* (Marburg: Elwert Verlag, 1965); Craig R. Koester, *Hebrews* (New York: Doubleday, 2001), 468–521. Here it is essential to respect the varying (six) accounts of "faith" offered by the NT (see n. 7

Hebrews uses *pistis* ("faith") thirty-two times and the corresponding verb, *pisteuein* ("to believe"), twice—not to mention near equivalents. This letter primarily understands faith to be the appropriate response to the "good news," or the "gospel." Craig Koester summarizes the way Hebrews envisages the genesis of faith: "Faith is called into being through the Word of God, who spoke through the prophets and a Son (1:1–2). The principal form of the divine word is that of a promise, which points to a future fulfilment" (e.g. 10:23; 11:11).[25] In detail, faith means hearing and receiving the gospel message (4:2–3), repenting of sin or "works that lead to death," having faith "toward God" (6:1), confidently drawing near to God (10:22), and trusting that God will reward those who seek him (11:6).

The only time that Hebrews indicates the object of faith comes in 6:1, where it is God (rather than Christ) who is the object of faith. Likewise it is God (rather than Christ, as in Matt 25:31–46) who "rewards those who seek him" (11:6). Unlike the letters of Paul and the Gospel of John (which present faith in a specifically Christological way) and the Synoptic Gospels (which, in a less reflective way, also present faith as faith in Jesus Christ), Hebrews tends to picture faith "theologically" rather than as a personal relationship to Jesus.

In several ways, the vision of faith provided by Paul, for instance, finds only a limited counterpart in Hebrews. First, for him it is the apostolic preaching of Jesus Christ that arouses faith (e.g. Rom. 10:14–17). By hearing and obeying "the word of Christ" (e.g. Rom. 10:17), human beings share in the redemption effected by his death and resurrection. Second, the Holy Spirit, who is "the Spirit of Christ" and "the Spirit of God," is actively involved when human beings come to faith (e.g. Rom. 8:9; 2 Cor. 3:6; Gal. 3:2). Third, Paul interprets faith as essentially justifying and salvific (e.g. Rom. 10:5–13). Forgiveness and justification set right a situation that has been destroyed

---

above). Unquestionably these accounts show family resemblances, but they should not be homogenized to produce "the" NT teaching on faith.

25. Koester, *Hebrews*, 125.

by sin (e.g. Rom. 4:25). These three particular perspectives on faith enjoy no clear parallels in Hebrews.[26]

It is in 11:1–12:2 that Hebrews invokes "faith" most emphatically; this passage contains twenty-five out of the thirty-two occurrences of *pistis* that we find in the letter. ("Faith" occurs only seven times elsewhere: 4:2; 6:1, 12; 10:22, 38, 39; 13:7). Given the chapter's emphasis on faith, not surprisingly it opens with a claim to "define" what faith is—proving itself, in fact, the only passage in the NT that attempts such a "definition": "faith is the assurance (*hypostasis*) of things hoped for, the conviction (*elenchos*) of things not seen" (NRSV).

This passage in Hebrews led St. Augustine and other fathers of the church to find here a definition of faith.[27] Saint Thomas Aquinas more or less followed suit by commenting that Hebrews 11:1 "describes" faith and gives "a complete but obscure definition" of faith (*Ad Hebreos*, 11.1.551–52). In his *Summa Theologiae* he stated that "the verse touches on all the elements whereby faith is definable," even if "it does not cast the words in definitional form" (IIa IIae 4.1). In the *Divine Comedy*, when Dante arrives in paradise, he is asked, "Faith, what is it?" He responds by quoting Hebrews 11:1 (Canto 24.52, 64) and presses on to explain faith in terms of what Aquinas had written.

Let us see the possibilities for the theology of religions offered by the "theological" (rather than "Christological") characteristics of faith set out in Hebrews 11:1–12:2. To be sure, this passage packs in many (biblical) heroes and heroines of faith who preceded Jesus and ends by proposing him, "the pioneer and perfecter of faith," as the supreme model for the Christian community to whom the letter has been sent. Nevertheless, the passage suggests ways to understand and interpret the faith of those who do not (or do not yet) receive the revelation conveyed through the Jewish-Christian message. When

---

26. For the differences between Paul's perspectives on faith and those of Hebrews, see Grässer, *Der Glaube im Hebräerbrief*, 64–71.

27. Augustine, *In Ioannem* 79.1; 85.2; Theodoret of Cyrrhus, *Interpretatio Epistolae ad Hebreos*, Patrologia Graeca 82, 757A.

Hebrews "defines" faith, it offers the possibility of looking beyond the biblical people of faith and applying the definition to those who believe in God through experiencing the witness of visible, created reality,[28] and through accepting some truth offered by their experience, their religious traditions, and their spiritual leaders.

The Faith of Others

Traditionally some have favored translating the opening account of faith (Heb. 11:1) subjectively and rendering the key words as the firm "certainty" and "conviction" or sure confidence of believers.[29] Sensitive to the basis for this confidence, others, however, take *hypostasis* as the objective reality of the good things (which constitute the heavenly world) that are hoped for, and *elenchos* as the objective proof or guarantee for what is not seen (the heavenly world), the evidence that produces conviction. Thus understanding both *hypostasis* and *elenchos* objectively, the Revised English Bible translates: "faith gives substance to our hopes and convinces us of realities we do not see."[30] The NRSV (see above), by rendering *hypostasis* as "assurance," takes advantage of the two possibilities this English word offers: "*objectively* it is a pledge or guarantee and *subjectively* it is a personal state of certainty," hope, or expectation.[31] In this interpretation the objective assurance of faith

---

28. Although often neglected, a speech made by Paul and Barnabas in Lystra proves its relevance: "the living God . . . made the heaven, the earth, the sea, and all that is in them . . . he has not left himself without witness in doing good, giving you rains from heaven and fruitful seasons, and filling you with food and your hearts with joy" (Acts 14:15, 17).

29. The general usage of *elenchos*, however, makes it difficult to follow the NRSV and interpret the term subjectively as personal conviction; see Walter Bauer, Frederick W. Danker, William T. Arndt, and F. Wilbur Gingrich, *A Greek-English Lexicon of the New Testament and Other Early Christian Literature*, 3rd ed. (Chicago: University of Chicago Press, 2000), 315.

30. See ibid., "*hypostasis*," 818–20.

31. Koester, *Hebrews*, 472; emphasis added.

comes from what is hoped for, just as the firm, personal assurance of faith *concerns what* is hoped for.[32]

The "objective" preference of the REB strengthens the case for the prior initiative of God's revealing and saving action, to which we come later. For the moment we need to bring together Hebrews 11:1 and 11:3 ("By faith we understand that the worlds were prepared by the Word of God, so that what is seen was made from things that are not visible"—NRSV).[33] Hebrews 11:1 and 11:3 present faith as looking both to the *origin* and to the *goal* of things. The reality of the visible world is there—before our eyes. But we do not see either its origin (in being fashioned by the divine word) or the future reward that we hope for (in response to God's promises). Yet the "unseen realities of God give proof of their existence by their power to evoke faith."[34] Faith is the bridge to the invisible reality of God, who as the unseen power has formed the things that we see and toward whom our hope reaches out in expectation. Thus faith relates believers not only to the existence of God's invisible world but also to a future not yet present.

Hebrews 11:2 speaks of "the elders" who "received approval" from God for their faith; some of those specified later in the chapter were Israelites (e.g. Abraham, Sarah, Isaac, and Jacob). Nevertheless, the chapter's roll call of heroes and heroines of faith opens with pre-Israelites (Abel, Enoch, and Noah; Heb. 11:4–7), and includes a later non-Israelite heroine, Rahab the prostitute (Heb. 11:31). All four represent, in general, human beings who receive approval from God, since they acted on the basis of faith, hoped in what God promised, and trusted that God would keep those promises about future things not yet "seen." By faith they also "understood" the unseen origin of the world to have been formed by the command of God. People of faith, whoever they were and are, recognize God in

---

32. Ibid., 473.
33. "By faith we understand that the universe was formed by God's command, so that the visible came forth from the invisible" (REB).
34. Koester, *Hebrews*, 480.

the genesis of the universe, just as they hope in God's promise about the goal of the world. Both in their understanding of the past and their hopes for the future, those who embrace faith are entwined with the life of the invisible God. Faith cannot prove the "unseen things" of God; rather faith itself is the "proof" of these things. The invisible power of God evokes faith and hope, and directs human beings toward invisible ends. Thus both the visible universe and human beings (through their faith) witness to the reality of the unseen power of God.

The account of faith provided by the opening verses of Hebrews 11 allows us to glimpse the human (and not merely Christian) questions to which faith supplies an answer. (1) Is there anything beyond the visible world? Are we bonded with things unseen or, rather, with the unseen God? (2) Where do we and our universe come from? Has "that which is seen" come into being "from that which cannot be seen": that is to say, from God and from God's creative command? We are born into a world that is not of our making. Do we nourish faith in the invisible Creator from whom all things have come? Such faith is close to gratitude toward the invisible Giver, a gratitude for the past from which we have emerged and for the future to which we are summoned. (3) Does it matter how we behave? Should we imitate our "ancestors," approved by God for their persevering faith? Should we live as pilgrims afflicted by various sufferings but always hoping for "a better country" (Heb. 11:16) and yearning for a God-given salvation to come? In short, may we and should we trust God as the one who "rewards those who seek him" (Heb. 11:6)?

Pleasing God

Such questions are not limited to Christians but arise for every human being and call them to faith. Hebrews 11:6 allows us to glimpse what such faith entails. As we saw above, Vatican II referred to this universal need for faith and specified only that it "pleases God," without explaining what that means (*AG* 7). We can unpack what "pleasing God" involves and then add three further items that Hebrews 11:6 also indicates by stating, "for whoever would approach him [God] must believe that he exists and that he rewards those who seek him" (NRSV).

(1) Subsequent exhortations in Hebrews fill out what "pleasing God" involves: Let us give thanks by which we offer God worship in a *pleasing* way with reverence and awe" (Heb. 13:16). A further passage summarizes such "pleasing God" in terms of doing the divine will: "May the God of peace . . . make you complete in everything good so that you may do his will, working among us that which is *pleasing* in his sight" (Heb. 13:20–21). We could sum up what this "pleasing God" intends: it envisages a faith that gratefully offers to God a reverent worship and does God's will through acts of kindness and service of others. Obviously, explicit faith in Christ should vigorously empower this life of faith. Yet a *vertical* relationship with God (through grateful worship and the "authentic prayer" mentioned above by Dupuis) and a *horizontal* relationship with other human beings (through self-sacrificing kindness) do not as such depend upon a conscious relationship with Christ. Hebrews does not say, "without faith in Christ it is impossible to please God." A faith that pleases God is open to those who have never heard of Christ.

(2) What "approaching" or "drawing near" to God involves is also explained by other passages in Hebrews. It means approaching God in prayer and worshiping God. Thus the anonymous author writes of "drawing near to the throne of grace" (Heb. 4:16; see 4:1–11; 10:19–22). Christian believers will be conscious of doing this through Jesus, "since he always lives to make intercession for them" (Heb. 7:25). But approaching God in prayer and worship does not demand an awareness that such "drawing near" depends on the priestly intercession of the risen and actively present Christ. His intercession is at work, whether or not worshipers are conscious of Christ when they approach God in prayer.

(3) Obviously those who draw near to God in prayer believe that God *exists*. They answer the question "is there anything or anyone beyond the visible world?" by bonding with the invisible God and somehow recognizing that God has entered into a gracious relationship with them (see Heb. 4:6). Their faith involves accepting that the world has been made by God, whom they worship as the unseen Creator, from whom all things have come, and toward whom all things are directed. God is both the origin and the goal of the world (Heb. 11:1, 3; see 2:10).

(4) In faith God is accepted not only as the origin of the universe but also as the one who "rewards those who seek him." This means letting God be the future goal of one's existence. God is trusted as just and faithful to his promises, however they are specifically understood and construed. In some way or another, those who embrace faith set themselves on a journey as pilgrims who hope for "a better country, that is, a heavenly one" (Heb. 11:16), and a future as yet unseen. Yet in Hebrews 11:6, the author does not specify what shape this reward will take, nor does he distinguish between rewards for his Christian readers[35] and for others "who seek" God. Without consciously intending this, he summons all God-seekers alike to put their future in the hands of the just and faithful God (see Heb. 10:23).

Suffering and Faith

Moving beyond these four reflections on Hebrews 11:6, we can see that this letter recognizes how those who in faith seek God not only do great things but also suffer great things. The pilgrimage of faith that directs them to the future reward

---

35. Elsewhere Hebrews speaks of Christians striving to enter God's "rest" (e.g. 4:1–11) and "looking for the city that is to come" (13:14), the city "whose architect and builder is God" (11:10). After speaking of Abraham, Sarah, Isaac, and Jacob, the author of Hebrews remarks that they all looked for a "homeland" or "a better country that is a heavenly one" (Heb. 11:13–16).

may involve severe suffering. Apropos of Hebrews 11:32–40, Koester remarks: "The text evokes associations with an ever widening circle of faithful people. The passage creates a collage of people and events from various periods, showing that what matters is not the time in which people live, but the faith that they exhibit."[36] The passage in Hebrews invites us to recognize the faithful *perseverance* of those who remain steadfast when faced with suffering. Koester's words could be modified to read: "The text evokes associations with an ever widening circle of faithful and suffering people. The passage creates a collage of people and events from various periods, showing that what matters is not the time in which people live, but the genuine faith, explicitly Christian or otherwise, they persevere in showing when confronted with great suffering and difficulty."

While Hebrews 11:32–40 explicitly refers to men and women remembered from the history of Israel, the verses apply also to all non-Israelites whose faith enables them to endure suffering and persevere in their pilgrimage to the divine rewards. They too are called to "run with perseverance the race set before" them by faith (Heb. 12:1). An appeal for perseverance made elsewhere applies also to them: "do not abandon that confidence of yours; it brings a great reward" (Heb. 10:35; see 10:23).

Suffering threads through the whole story of the witnesses to faith: from Abel, the man of faith killed by his brother (Heb. 11:4) to Jesus himself, "the pioneer and perfecter of faith" who "endured the cross" (Heb. 12:2).[37] The murdered Abel and the crucified Jesus bracket the list of witnesses; shortly after that, the text returns to the "sprinkled blood" of Abel and Jesus (Heb. 12:24). Noah was threatened by a catastrophic flood (Heb. 11:7); Abraham, Sarah, Isaac, and Jacob lived in tents, as displaced persons "in a foreign land" (Heb. 11:9); "all of these

---

36. Koester, *Hebrews*, 516–17.
37. On the faith of Jesus, see G. O'Collins, *Christology: A Biblical, Historical, and Systematic Study of Jesus*, 2nd ed. (Oxford: Oxford University Press, 2009), 260–80.

died in faith," as "strangers and foreigners on earth" (Heb. 11:13); Abraham suffered for his faith by being tested through being commanded to offer Isaac as a sacrifice (Heb. 11:17). Hebrews sets out at length what Moses suffered for faith (Heb. 11:23–28). After recalling what the faith of Gideon and others involved (Heb. 11:32–34), Hebrews commends "for their faith" what a cloud of witnesses suffered through torture, imprisonment, execution (by the sword, stoning, and being "sawn in two"), destitution, and homelessness (Heb. 11:35–39).

Without laboring the conclusion, Hebrews reports various forms of suffering that embracing faith entails. It lets us gain a sense of the mysterious link between suffering and faith. Whoever believers are and wherever they are found in the human story, the history of faith, right from the mythical beginning with Cain and Abel, is stamped with suffering. As we might say in light of Hebrews 12:2, "outside the cross there is no faith" (*extra crucem nulla fides*).

The Faith of Christians and the Faith of Others

Drawing on Hebrews 11:1–12:2 to fashion an account of the faith of "others" leaves us with the challenge of facing the differences between the faith of Christians and that of others. Let us begin by specifying three such differences that emerge when we compare and contrast the passage from Hebrews with other NT witnesses.

Paul's vision of the move to faith includes repentance from sin (for instance, by turning away from "idols" [1 Thess. 1:9]), the action of the Holy Spirit (e.g. Gal. 3:2), and entering a new community, the Body of Christ (e.g. Gal. 3:23–29). Our passage from Hebrews remains silent about these three features that characterize the genesis of faith; it neither affirms nor denies them. It simply does not say that "without a faith that turns away from sin, obeys the promptings of the Holy Spirit, and joins a community of faith, it is impossible to please God." We recognize here some limits in the teaching of Hebrews, rather than genuine difficulties against applying this teaching to the case of religious "others." What Hebrews does state, however, provides difficulties in two areas: (1) the trigger of faith and (2) its content.

First, on the basis of such items as God's warning to Noah and call to Abraham (Heb. 11:7, 8), Koester maintained: "the unseen realities [of God] are made known through divine revelation, including promises, commands, and warnings" and "revelation is received by faith."[38] Since human faith responds to divine revelation and exists only as a response to revelation, what about those to whom no such "promises, commands and warnings" come? In the light of Hebrews 11:1 and 2, Koester should have added something: the divine revelation that makes known the unseen realities of God *also* includes the witness of "what is seen." This witness, while not constituting a command or warning, also conveys the promise of unseen things that we "hope for." This witness and promise form a revelation of God that invites human beings, whoever they are, to embrace faith and continue steadfastly the journey of faith. Hence Hebrews allows or even encourages us to acknowledge how, in the case of the nonevangelized, their faith also exists as a response to divine revelation.

The content of faith (*fides quae*) may pose a more troublesome question. Hebrews, after all, insists on a Christian "confession" (Heb. 10:23) that accepts that Jesus is the Son of God (Heb. 4:14), the heir of all things (Heb. 1:1-5), and "the apostle and high priest of our confession'" (Heb. 3:1). The content of faith for those who do not (or do not yet) share the Christian confession lacks such specificity. It involves simply believing that God exists and is a just, life-giving power who promises a mysterious future to those who believe in him (Heb. 11:1, 3, 6).

Such a marked difference (along with a partial similarity) at the level of content will worry those who look for a more or less uniform content of faith. This is apparently what Aquinas wanted to argue. He claimed that, even though the gospel had not yet been proclaimed, the Israelites enjoyed essentially the

---

38. Koester, *Hebrews*, 100.

same faith (in the sense of *fides quae*) as Christians, since the real object of their confession was the same. On the basis of Hebrews 11:6, Aquinas maintained that belief in God's existence and rewards constituted the primary, essential content of faith. By holding this faith, the Israelites implicitly grasped the entire revealed mystery of God, and hence could be seen to have already enjoyed essentially the same faith as (later) Christians.[39]

Instead of this "leveling" of the content of faith down to the lowest common denominator, I propose an alternative that allows for variations in the *fides quae*. In what they confessed about God revealed in history and creation, there were and are similarities and differences between devout Israelites and Christians. There is no need to argue, for instance, that the faith of Abraham, Sarah, Moses, Rahab, and the prophets was essentially, if implicitly, the same as that of Christians responding to the good news of Jesus' life, death, resurrection, ascension, and gift of the Holy Spirit.

Moreover, within the history of Israel itself we observe growth in the content of the confession of faith. Creeds of Israel confessed the revelation of God through divine acts in the history of the chosen people:

> A wandering Aramean was my ancestor; he went down to Egypt and lived there as an alien, few in number, and there he became a great nation, mighty and populous. When the Egyptians treated us harshly and affected us, by imposing hard labor on us, we cried to the Lord, the God of our ancestors. The Lord heard our voice and saw our affliction, our toil and our oppression. The Lord brought us out of Egypt with a mighty hand and an outstretched arm, with a terrifying display of power, and with signs and wonders, and he brought us to this place and gave us this land, a land flowing with milk and honey. (Deut. 26:5–9; see 6:20–25; Josh. 24:2–13)

---

39. *Summa Theologiae*, IIa IIae 1.7.

Hebrews 11 lists Abel, Enoch, Noah, Abraham, Sarah, Isaac, and Jacob among the ancient exemplars of faith, but none of them could share in the confession of faith we find in Deuteronomy and Joshua. The liberation from suffering in Egypt and the entrance into "a land flowing with milk and honey" had not yet taken place.

Paul holds Abraham up as the great model of faith (Rom. 4:1–22). However, "our father in faith," while he obeyed God's commands and trusted God's promises in an exemplary way (Heb. 11:8–12), embraced a *fides quae* that was considerably "less" than and somewhat different from that of later Jews and future Christians. He could not, for instance, accept in faith the resurrection of Jesus Christ from the dead (Rom. 10:8–10); it had not yet occurred. The content of faith (*fides quae*) for Abraham and Sarah was in important respects unlike that accepted by the followers of Jesus. It was the "obedience" (*fides qua*) of Abraham and Sarah that brought them closer to the faith of committed Christians. Thus it was much more his obedient *fides qua* than his *fides quae* that made Abraham "our father in faith" and the "father in faith" for all faithful human beings.

Obedience and the Divine Initiative

The roll call of heroes and heroines of faith in Hebrews 11 introduces only once the theme of "obedience." It does so when expounding the central example of Abraham: "by faith Abraham obeyed when he was called to set out for a place that he was to receive as an inheritance; and he set out not knowing where he was going" (Heb. 11:8). Elsewhere, obedience shows up as a key feature in the plot of Hebrews, not least when it portrays the prayer and obedience of Jesus himself. By obediently submitting to the divine will and dying, he "became the source [or cause] of eternal salvation for all who obey him" (5:7–9). Thus the faithful obedience of Jesus became God's way for saving human beings.

But where does that leave all those innumerable outsiders who do not know Jesus and hence cannot consciously obey him and experience in him the cause or source of their eternal salvation? This question can be met by observing a qualification that Hebrews introduces into the drama of human salvation. We may presume that the "great cloud of witnesses" (Heb. 12:1) cited, either by name or in general, in Hebrews 11, were eventually blessed with eternal salvation. Yet they all existed before Christ and could not have consciously obeyed him. If they had known him, they would presumably have obeyed him. Yet they did not know him. The same is true of innumerable "outsiders," whose faith enabled and enables them to "please" God. Without knowing Jesus and hence without the possibility of consciously obeying him and of "looking to" him as the supreme exemplar in the "race" of faith (Heb. 12:1–2), they mysteriously experience him (and his Holy Spirit) as the cause of their salvation. The faith they can exercise does not include conscious obedience toward Jesus, but that does not prevent him from being the effective "pioneer of their salvation" (Heb. 2:10).

Obedience, whether conscious or unconscious, responds to the divine initiative. Above we cited Irenaeus on the prior initiative of God in matters of revelation and salvation: "No one can know God unless God teaches [him or her]; without God, God is not to be known." Hebrews 11 points to the prior activity of God in rousing faith. By calling faith "the assurance of things hoped for," our text implies prior promises being somehow communicated by God and evoking the response of human hope. By naming faith as "the proof of things not seen," Hebrews suggests the unseen reality of God that gives proof of its existence by its power to call forth faith. The prior divine initiative applies not only to the Israelites and Christians but also to all those "others" who respond in faith to God's self-communication.

Conclusion

This chapter moved beyond the question of salvation for those who follow other faiths and examined a possible biblical approach to their responding in *faith* to the divine self-revelation. Standard scriptural dictionaries illustrate how faith is a diversified reality and assumes at least six forms in the NT. The Second Vatican Council's decree on missionary activity (*AG* 7) pointed to one of these forms—in Hebrews 11:6 ("without faith it is impossible to please God")— and applied it to the faith possibilities for the religious "others." In fact, the whole section of Hebrews 11:1–12:2 illuminates what their faith could be: a *fides qua,* or commitment of hopeful obedience, and a *fides quae,* or content that accepts God as the origin and goal of human living but does not include any explicitly Christological component.

Hebrews does not say: "without (explicit) faith in Christ it is impossible to please God." A faith that "pleases God" is open to those suffering human beings who have never explicitly heard of Christ and his message.

6

Discerning the Presence
of Christ and the Spirit

In its Declaration on the Relation of the Church to Non-Christian Religions (*Nostra Aetate*), the Second Vatican Council stated that "the Catholic Church rejects nothing of those things that are *true and holy* in the other religions. She has a sincere respect for those [other] manners of acting and living, those precepts and doctrines that, although differing in many ways from what she herself holds and proposes, nevertheless, often reflect a *ray of that Truth that enlightens all human beings*" (*NA* 2; emphasis mine). Even if the text included no explicit biblical reference, it obviously echoed the language of the prologue to St. John's Gospel about the Word being "the light of human beings" (John 1:4), "the true light that enlightens everyone" (John 1:9). *Nostra Aetate* points us in the opposite direction: not from the Word to human beings but from them to the Word. The other religions, through their teachings and practice, often reflect something of the Light that is the divine Word.

Justin, Vatican II, and John Paul II

From the second century the Johannine discourse about the Word being the Truth and Light of the world fed into what Justin Martyr and his successors (Irenaeus, Clement of Alexandria, Origen, Athanasius, Augustine, and others) said about the impact of the Word on all human beings. In his *First Apology*, a work addressed to Roman authorities who were persecuting Christians, Justin wrote: "we have been taught that Christ is the first begotten of God and that he is the Word (Logos) in whom the whole human race partakes. *Those who have lived according to the Word are Christians*, even though they have been considered atheists: such as, among the Greeks, Socrates, Heraclitus, and others like them." Turning his gaze from past philosophers to the present, Justin called "Christians" not only "those who lived then" but also those "who live now according to reason" (46; italics mine).[1]

In developing the Johannine theme of the preexistent Logos as universal mediator of creation and revelation, Justin spoke of "the seeds of the Word" that have been dropped everywhere and, at least to some extent, in every person (*Second Apology* 8.10.13). He argued that, in one way or another, the whole human race shares in the Logos (*First Apology* 46). Many people live only "according to a fragment of the Logos." Christians live "according to the knowledge and contemplation of the whole Logos, who is Christ" (*Second Apology* 8). While claiming to know "in virtue of his own grace" the incarnate Logos "who is from the unbegotten and ineffable God," Justin and other Christians did not deny some presence and impact ("the seeds of the Logos") in the life and thought of Plato, the Stoics, poets, and various prose authors—an impact that made their teachings, albeit only in certain respects, identical with those of Christ (*Second Apology* 13).[2]

Vatican II retrieved the language of John's Gospel (see also above) and Justin in its Decree on the Church's Missionary Activity. It recognized "elements of truth and grace" found everywhere in the lives of individuals and the cultures of peoples, which are not to be discarded but rather "purged of evil associations" (*AG* 9). "The seeds of the Word" are "hidden"

---

1. See *Writings of Saint Justin Martyr,* trans. Thomas B. Falls (Washington, DC: Catholic University of America, 1948).

2. On Justin and his successors, see G. O'Collins, *The Second Vatican Council on Other Religions* (Oxford: Oxford University Press, 2013), 16–22.

in "the national and religious traditions" of various peoples. It is God who has "hidden," "distributed," and "sown" these "riches" (*AG* 11).[3]

In his first encyclical (1979), *Redemptor Hominis* (Redeemer of Human Beings), John Paul II cited *Nostra Aetate* as being "filled with deep esteem for the great spiritual values, indeed for the primacy of the spiritual, which in the life of human-kind finds expression in religion and then in morality." He also referred to what *Ad Gentes* had expounded on "the seeds of the Word": "The fathers of the church rightly saw in the various religions, as it were, so many reflections of the one truth, 'seeds of the Word,' attesting that, although the routes taken may be different, there is but a single goal to which are directed the deepest aspirations of the human spirit as expressed in its quest for God" (*RH* 11).

Mixing images in this dense statement (shining reflections, growing seeds, and routes taken), the pope made three points: (a) as *Ad Gentes* had already stated, in some sense the Word of God is present "in the various religions"; (b) the routes taken by these religions may differ but the goal (God) remains the same; and (c) the religions express the human "quest for God." How (a) happens (through the work of the Holy Spirit) was to be explained in a later encyclical, *Redemptoris Missio* (The Mission of the Redeemer) of 1990 (see below). Apropos of (b), the centrality given to Christ right through *Redemptor Hominis* shows that the pope did not endorse the view that the different "routes" are equally efficacious in bringing believers to their common goal in God. (c) John Paul II unquestionably assigned the priority to the divine initiative of Christ "entering the heart" of all human beings, who thus from the time of their conception share in "the mystery of redemption" (*RH* 8, 13).

In *Redemptoris Missio* John Paul II insisted, as we saw in Chapter 3, that, while manifested "in a special way in the Church and her members," the Holy Spirit's "presence and activity" are, nevertheless, "universal." He went on to say that

---

3. On the "seeds of the Word," see also *AG* 15 and 18.

"the Spirit's presence and activity affect not only individuals but also society and history, peoples, *cultures, and religions*" (*RM* 28; italics mine).

All this teaching from the fathers of the church, Vatican II, and John Paul II invites Christians to discern where the "seeds of the Word" or the "presence and activity" of the Holy Spirit are to be identified in the religious traditions of other living faiths. A document published jointly on May 19, 1991, by the Pontifical Council for Interreligious Dialogue and the Congregation for the Evangelization of Peoples, "Dialogue and Proclamation," highlighted the need to discern what it called "elements of grace" in other religious traditions (art. 30, 82; ND 1060, 1065).[4] What criteria could be available to guide this process of discernment and verify the presence of such "elements of grace," both in the religions themselves and in the cultures and history in which they are inseparably embedded?

Such a task of discerning this presence obviously belongs to the job description of a work on the Christology of religions. Official teaching has maintained the presence of Christ and his Spirit. *Gaudium et Spes*, for instance, taught: "Constituted Lord by his resurrection and given all power in heaven and on earth, Christ is already at work through the power of his Spirit in the hearts of human beings, not only arousing a desire for the world to come but also enlivening, purifying, and strengthening the generous desires of humankind" (*GS* 38). Where an earlier article highlighted the activity of the Holy Spirit in joining people to the crucified and risen Christ (*GS* 22), this article "reverses" the roles and portrays Christ acting through the Spirit and doing so in the hearts of all human beings, whatever their religious adherence or lack of such adherence. Either way, we are left with the challenge of discerning the presence and activity of Christ and his Spirit in various religions and beyond.

The theology of Karl Rahner also leaves us with this challenge. He writes of "Jesus Christ present and operative in

---

4. The full text is available in the *Bulletin of the Council for Interreligious Dialogue* 77/26 (1991/92): 210–50.

non-Christian religions" and this happening "in and through his Spirit."[5] What then are the signs of this presence and operation?

Four Criteria for Discerning the Presence of the Word and the Spirit

What criteria might we employ to identify in Buddhism, Hinduism, Islam, and other living faiths and in the lives of those who follow these faiths the "seeds of the Word," the presence and activity of the Holy Spirit, "elements of grace," or however we care to name the creative, revealing, and redeeming presence of Christ and his Spirit? To investigate criteria for carrying through this discernment amounts to searching for authentic religious experiences that shape prayer and action and attest the presence of Christ and the Spirit. In Chapter 3 above, we recalled what John Paul II said on December 22, 1986, about authentic prayer: "every authentic prayer is called forth by the Holy Spirit." We could expand this criterion into four criteria for identifying experiences that are authentically religious—in the sense of putting followers of various religions genuinely in touch with God and, religiously, in touch with other human beings.

First, authentically religious experiences can be expected to manifest a certain *profundity* that goes deeper than the shallow flux of everyday experiences. In situations of solitude, danger, surprise, joy, and so forth, people can be carried beneath the superficial level of ordinary experience to sense two things at the heart of their lives: on the one hand, their radical weakness, finitude, and dependence, and, on the other hand, some meaning and strength that is given to them. In such episodes people, whether they are followers of living faiths or of none at all, know something of their absolute need and final values, even when the deepest reality is not explicitly identified

---

5. K. Rahner, *Foundations of Christian Faith* (New York: Seabury Press, 1978), 315, 316.

as God. In short, an authentically religious experience has a
certain depth to it.

This first criterion for assessing religious experience reso-
nates with one dimension of faith as presented in Hebrews
11, which we recalled in the last chapter. Faith answers the
question: Is there anything beyond the visible world? Are we
bonded with things unseen, or, rather, with the unseen God?
Experiences that respond positively to the question by taking
people of various religions beyond the merely visible to the
very heart of their lives can be judged "authentic," in the sense
of genuinely putting them in touch with the invisible God.

Second, genuine religious experiences will do more than
simply jolt people into sensing the ultimate dimensions of
human existence. Such experiences will *modify subsequent activity.* What has been consciously and profoundly experienced
may be expected to have *consequences* that change the lives of
people. Such changes can take the two basic forms of *hope* and
love.

An authentic religious experience, whether precisely identified as such or not, means encountering the God "who is and
who was and who *is to come*" (Rev. 1:8). This expression from
the Book of Revelation gives the divine "futurity" a special
prominence. It implies that God will be truly and fully God
for us only when the life of the final, divine kingdom comes. A
genuine experience of God should encourage a basically hopeful stance toward life, even if this experience does not formally
lead to a clear belief about life beyond death. It was the kind of
experience attributed to Abraham, Sarah, and other friends of
God in the early stages of Israelite history when explicit belief
in resurrection from the dead had not yet emerged. Those
who, like them, have been touched by the living God (who in
fact holds out to all human beings a full future beyond death)
will somehow embody in their subsequent activity the conviction: We are not facing an inevitable betrayal; existence is not
inherently disappointing and finally absurd.

Once again a criterion for recognizing authentic religious
experience corresponds to a central aspect of faith provided

by Hebrews 11. That chapter encourages the faith of those who live as pilgrims, afflicted by various sufferings but always hoping for "a better country" (Heb. 11:16) and yearning for a salvation to come from God "who rewards those who seek him" (Heb. 11:6).

Alongside signs of a fundamentally hopeful attitude, genuine religious experience should induce care, compassion, and a generous openness to the needs of others. Any such experience will develop responsible *love*. Zen Buddhism deploys ten images to explain the nature of *satori,* or profound illumination. The last image shows a man walking along a road into a city. The point is clear. One who has been genuinely illuminated will seek out other people and help them enjoy the same kind of precious illumination.

This criterion of a loving openness to the needs of others also enjoys its counterpart in the vision of faith proffered by Hebrews. The faith that "pleases" God does the divine will through acts of kindness and service to others (Heb. 13:20–21). Where religious experience leads to such self-sacrificing kindness, we are justified in acknowledging the experience as authentically engaged with God.

In short, this second criterion looks beyond the profound quality of religious experiences to observe the hopeful and loving "behavior modifications" that such experiences bring in their wake.

Third, in the last chapter we saw how Jacques Dupuis linked authentic religious experience with Jesus Christ: "Wherever there is genuine religious experience, it is surely the God revealed in Jesus Christ who thus enters into the lives of men and women, in a hidden secret fashion."[6] Here Dupuis rightly reminds us that there can be no substitute for testing supposed "seeds of the Word" against God's self-communication in Jesus Christ. Authentic religious experiences can be expected to be *somehow Christological*—that is to say, to display features

---

6. J. Dupuis, *Christianity and the Religions: From Confrontation to Dialogue* (Maryknoll, NY: Orbis Books, 2002), 122.

that hint at the creative, revealing, and redeeming presence of Christ. This criterion requires that the religious experiences in question exhibit traces of his presence and power, or what we might call the *semina Verbi* or the *vestigia Christi* (the footprints of Christ). To do so, we need to recall (a) creation, (b) the history of Jesus, (c) his crucifixion, and (d) his resurrection from the dead that initiated an explosion of Spirit-prompted life.

Creation

The NT amply acknowledges the role of Christ in creation: "all things were created through him and for him. He is before all things, and in him all things hold together" (Col. 1:16–17; see John 1:1–4; Heb. 1:3; 1 Cor. 8:6). Despite their different nuances, all these witnesses agree that through Christ all things came into being. They acknowledge him as the universal agent of creation who preserves everything in existence. The teaching of the NT supports a conclusion that is significant for this chapter. Whenever the created world and its history brings people revelation or salvation in some form or another, this happens through Christ. Seen in these terms, his role as mediator of revelation and salvation is as broad and as old as creation itself.

Those early Christian writers who took up the Johannine language about the Word of God dwelt on the universal revelatory role of the creative Word. Thus Irenaeus of Lyons wrote: "The Word of God, present with his handiwork from the beginning, reveals the Father to all, to whom he wills, when he wills, and how the Father wills" (*Adversus Haereses* 4.6.7). A little later Irenaeus added: "Through the Word all his creatures learn that there is one God, the Father, who controls all things and gives existence to all. . . . The Son makes the Father known from the beginning" (ibid., 4.20.6–7). When followers of other faiths reflect deeply on creation and experience it religiously, they can sense something of the creative Word present everywhere. Then their experience will mirror at least something of the omnipresent Word.

The followers of other religions and, indeed, all human beings experience a universe that presents itself as rule-governed, "obeying" everywhere the basic "laws of nature." Despite theories of chaos and the radical indeterminacy expressed by quantum theory, the discoveries of astronomy and the biological sciences have encouraged an awareness of a "rational" universe, finely tuned for the emergence of carbon-based life and of human beings. Here, of course, I could indulge a huge parenthesis in defense of a primordial "rationality" of creation, a view that resembles ancient beliefs about the Logos governing the universe. Let me simply state that religious "others" can display some awareness of a "rational" universe created, sustained, and governed by the Logos, even if they use different words to say this.

Athanasius of Alexandria, as we recalled in Chapter 1, saw the creation of the world and the incarnation of the Word as forming together one act of divine self-bestowal. The creative Word of God is also the deifying Word. All creatures exist by sharing the Word in the Holy Spirit and so participating in deification. As Athanasius put matters, "the Father creates and renews all things through the Word and the Spirit" (*Letter to Serapion* 1.24). To the extent that "other" believers experience and express such a consciousness of all things being formed by divine self-bestowal, we may recognize the presence of Christ and his Spirit at work in them.

Since God created humankind in the Word or *Logos*, this allowed Athanasius to introduce an interesting pun: the human being is *logikos*, which means both "rational" and "made according to the Logos" (*De Incarnatione* 3). Hence, human beings cannot truly understand who they are unless they do so in the light of the Word. Since God created us in the Word, we must be images of Christ, the perfect Image of the Father. Humankind can reach a full knowledge of itself only through, with, and in Christ. "The Word of God came in his own person," Athanasius concluded, "so that, as he was the Image of the Father, he could create afresh human beings after the image" (ibid. 13.7). This Athanasian insight contributes to the scope of this chapter. Insofar as any human beings, Christian and "others" alike, show that in some way they understand themselves as rational beings created in the image of God, they manifest at least a dim awareness of the creative Word.

As the beautiful Word, Wisdom, or Image of God, Christ lets his beauty shine everywhere. Gerard Manley Hopkins (1844–89) celebrated this universally present beauty. In his poem "As Kingfishers Catch Fire," he wrote: "for Christ plays in ten thousand places,/Lovely in limbs, and lovely in eyes not his/ To the Father through the features of men's face." Looking at human beings anywhere and everywhere, one might well join Hopkins and say: "Where there is beauty, there is Christ" (*ubi pulchritudo ibi Christus*). Those (whoever they are) who experience other human beings as beautiful are in fact experiencing something of the beauty of Christ, the unique Image of God. We can discern the presence of Christ in their experience of beauty.

The History of Jesus

Moving beyond creation, we come to the religious experiences, practices, and teachings of various religions that display similarities to central items in *the gospel message*. In Chapter 1, we commented on Jesus' love command, which drew together love of God and love of neighbor. Jesus distinguished but would not separate the vertical relationship to God and the horizontal relationship to one's neighbor. Together they form one commitment of love that transcends all other commitments in importance. While Jesus innovated here in a startling way (see Chap. 1), nevertheless, we find similar teachings and practices in other religions. It is a commonplace to observe how love is central to all living faiths.

In Chapter 1, we noted a certain convergence between the teaching of Jesus on the norms for final judgment and what we find elsewhere. Ulrich Luz points out how the "catalogue of charitable works" found in Matthew 25:31–46 converges with "statements from other religions." This list "appears in similar language in other religions," and, one should add, also in the Old Testament and further Jewish sources.[7] Unquestionably, Jesus did something unique when he identified himself with the hungry, the sick, those in jail, refugees, and others who suffer. Nevertheless, the "charitable works" proposed for the practice of "other" believers reflect and parallel, at least partially, what the Truth incarnate taught. In such ethical codes we may discern the "seeds of the Word" at work.

The Crucifixion

The story of Jesus' passion includes the precious detail that he did not die alone. At the place called Golgotha two others were crucified with him (Mark 15:27 parr.). Like all men and women, Christians and non-Christians alike, those criminals had two things in common with Jesus: *their bodies and their sufferings.* We can differ from Jesus in sex, age, race, language, culture, and our period in history. But everyone has a body and sufferings, and that creates a radical solidarity between Jesus and all human beings. When Jesus "suffered outside the gate," in a profane, nonsacred place (Heb. 13:12), his passion made him part of that total story of ordinary and extraordinary suffering endured by men and women in the course of their daily lives. The two criminals crucified with Jesus symbolized the whole history of suffering, which stretches from the beginning to the end, when "God will wipe away every tear from their eyes, and death shall be no more. Neither shall there be mourning nor crying nor pain any more, for the former things have passed away" (Rev. 21:4).

Right from Chapter 1, this book has endorsed the principle "where there is suffering, there is Christ" (*ubi dolor, ibi Christus*). Human beings, no matter what their religious persuasion, suffer everywhere. As Jesus himself implied in his vision of the Last Judgment (Matt. 25:31–46), the face of everyone who

---

7. U. Luz, *Matthew 21–28* (Minneapolis: Fortress Press, 2005), 266 n. 30, 269–70, 278 n. 137.

suffers deprivation is his face. In a particular way, those who are tortured and murdered share his passion and reveal the truth of the dictum we have quoted from Pascal (Chap. 1): "He is in agony until the end of the world." Wherever we look, we can see the crucified face of God.

During the Second World War and shortly after the horrors of the Spanish Civil War and Mussolini's invasion of Ethiopia, David Gascoyne (1916–2001), someone who endured the pain of mental illness, took up Pascal's thought and wrote a remarkable poem vividly picturing a world ravaged by the "sovereign lords" of fear and greed: "Ecce Homo." Gascoyne understood the victims of his times to be fellow sufferers of the crucified Jesus: "And on his either side hang dead/A laborer and a factory hand,/Or one is maybe a lynched Jew/And one a Negro or a Red,/Coolie or Ethiopian,/Spaniard or Christian democrat." Such victims, whether they knew this or not, succeeded the two men crucified with Jesus and constitute *vestigia Christi*, traces or imprints of the Calvary Christ in our world.

In one way or another, those who follow some religious faith—and, in fact, all human beings—share in the passion of Christ. The "seeds of the Word," which Justin acknowledged to be present everywhere, are seeds of "the crucified Word." Often showing a sensitivity that some theologians lack, modern artists such as Francis Bacon (1909–92), Marc Chagall (1897–1985), Sir Jacob Epstein (1880–1959), and others let us glimpse the face of the crucified Christ. A Christology of the religions dare not ignore the tragic Christ, there to be experienced and acknowledged in the whole history of human suffering, whether it is the suffering of individuals or of groups, like the Yazidis in Syria, who face persecution, forced conversion, or even genocidal massacre.[8] Their experiences of suffering are latter-day intimations of the crucified Christ.

---

8. See David Brown, "The Incarnation in Twentieth-Century Art," in S. T. Davis, D. Kendall, and G. O'Collins (eds.), *The Incarnation: An Interdisciplinary Symposium on the Incarnation of the Son of God* (Oxford: Oxford

The Resurrection

By his resurrection, the Son of God, who was already through his incarnation "united in a certain way with every human being" (*GS* 22), became gloriously present through his new life with all people of all times and places. Endless signs of new life coming through death reproduced the pattern of the Easter mystery. The living presence of the risen Christ went hand in hand with what Bishop John Taylor called the Holy Spirit's "creative-redemptive action at the heart of everything" (Chap. 3 above). Here once again Christology and pneumatology go hand in hand. The new life of the resurrection coincides with the new life empowered by the Spirit.

Hopkins attended to both: in "The Windhover" he evoked the presence of Christ our risen Lord; but in "God's Grandeur" he also evoked "the dearest freshness" found "deep down things," because "the Holy Ghost over the bent/World broods with warm breast and with ah! bright wings." Those two poems suggest how religious experiences could point to the presence of the risen Christ and his life-giving Spirit.

Whatever the precise form involved, religious experiences that originate from God show forth some orientation toward Christ and his Spirit. Yet, to return to the task of identifying experiences that are authentically religious, the fourth and final criterion is that the divine self-communication in Christ bears a *trinitarian face*. Right from the writings of St. Paul (e.g. 2 Cor. 13:13), the first followers of Christ expressed their faith in God in a triune way. There was and is no God apart from the Father, the Son, and the Holy Spirit. We should expect some trinitarian shape in the religious experiences that come to human beings, both historically and in their meeting with the world of nature, even if the *vestigia Trinitatis* (the imprints

---

University Press, 2002), 332–72. While foregrounding "incarnation" in its title, this article has much to say about the crucifixion in modern art.

of the Trinity) become recognizable as such only in the light of Christian faith.

What is at stake here is not so much the primordial trinitarian shape of the universe that Thomas Aquinas adverts to when he writes of the Trinity being represented in human beings also "by means of an image" (*per modum imaginis*) and in other creatures only "by means of an imprint" (*per modum vestigii*).[9] Such talk about an *imago* or a *vestigium* of the Trinity belongs to the self-communication of God that forms the a priori condition for all human experience. This holds true also of Augustine's "psychological" theory of the Trinity. He saw all human knowledge and love as imaging forth the two processes by which the Father's act of thinking generates the Son, with the Holy Spirit as the mutual love between Father and Son. Here again we deal with what constitutes the a priori condition for the possibility of any human experience.

Our question is rather: Where in conscious, concrete experiences and their expression do we come across genuine signs of the Trinity's presence and operation? Our search presupposes that, despite all the failures due to human depravity and misinterpretation, we will find traces of the Trinity. Wherever God is and is experienced, there is the Trinity (*ubi Deus ibi Trinitas*). Thus we can anticipate that, in some way or another, authentic experiences of the divine reality and their expression will bear a trinitarian face.

Examples suggest themselves for examination: the Trimurti or Hindu triad representing three aspects of the Absolute Spirit (Brahma, Vishnu, and Siva); the *saccidananda* of Hindu mysticism (being, awareness of being, and enjoyment of being);[10] the Yin, Yang, and Tao of Taoism; and other religious experiences that speak of (a) the absolute origin of things, (b) some prin-

9. See Jean-Pierre Torrell, *Saint Thomas Aquinas* (Washington, DC: Catholic University of America Press, 2003), 2:80–82, 86, 88–92, 99, 115, and 343 on "image," and 2:65, 86 on "vestige."

10. See J. Dupuis, *Toward a Christian Theology of Religious Pluralism* (Maryknoll, NY: Orbis Books, 1997), 274–79.

ciple of order and meaning, and (c) the unity of love. My aim here, however, is not to indulge an enormous parenthesis and draw out several examples in great detail but rather to point to a possibility: *vestigia Trinitatis* can alert us to the presence of experiences that truly originate in the triune God.

Modern physics has championed a sense of the relationality of the material world. There is, as John Polkinghorne argues, "a satisfying degree of consonance discernible between the relationality of the physical world and the trinitarian character of its Creator." He writes:

> Physics has learned that Reality is Relational. This will come as no surprise to Trinitarian theologians, who have long believed in Being as Communion. [Polkinghorne cites John Zizioulas, *Being as Communion* (Crestwood, NY: St. Vladimir's Seminary Press, 1985).] Christian thinkers can perceive the intrinsic interconnectedness of the created universe as being a kind of pale reflection of the relatedness of the perichoretic exchange of love between the three Divine Persons in the Godhead.[11]

Scientific discoveries, human history, and experiences of all kinds throw up hints of the trinitarian character of God. Developing, for instance, the analogy of love, Richard of St. Victor (d. 1173) interpreted God as an absolute communion of love: in a movement from self-love, to mutual love, and on to shared love, or the Lover, the Beloved, and Equal Friend who supplied the inspiration for Brian Wren's hymn "How Wonderful the Three-in-One."[12] To the extent that, in their thinking

---

11. John Polkinghorne, "Some Light from Physics," in G. O'Collins and M. A. Myers, *Light from Light: Scientists and Theologians in Dialogue* (Grand Rapids, MI: Eerdmans, 2012), 17–27, at 25.

12. See G. O'Collins, *The Tripersonal God: Understanding and Interpreting the Trinity*, 2nd ed. (Mahwah, NJ: Paulist Press, 2014), 202–3; and Richard of St. Victor, *On the Trinity*, trans. Angelici Ruben (Eugene, OR: Cascade Books, 2011).

and/or in their deeper experiences, religious "others" (and those who follow no religious faith at all) sense the triune God who creates and sustains the world, we may discern in that something of the *vestigia Trinitatis* or even the *imago Trinitatis*

Conclusion

Such then are four criteria that serve to identify experiences that hint at the presence and activity of the risen Christ and the Holy Spirit: the criteria of *profundity*, of *appropriate consequences in behavior*, of *Christological and pneumatological orientation*, and of *trinitarian shape*. These criteria ask: Do the experiences in question reveal ultimate, absolute elements at the heart of human existence? Do they modify subsequent behavior and make it more hopeful and more loving? Do they disclose any orientation toward and impulse from Christ and his Spirit? Do they bear any *vestigia Trinitatis*? The first, third, and fourth criteria look directly at the experience itself. Is it profound, Christological or pneumatological, and in any way trinitarian? The second criterion focuses on the aftermath of the experience. Does it bring ethical consequences that are positively acceptable?

In applying these criteria, if we succumb to the impulse to investigate only the teachings of Buddhism, Hinduism, and other religions, we might be tempted to dismiss a great deal as deviant doctrine that fails to yield any signs of the revealing and saving presence of Christ and his Spirit. The difficulty could be eased if we shift the focus a little from the spoken and written expressions of religious experience to consider also the nonverbal expressions and, of course, the experiences themselves in their concrete reality.

In the case of Christian teaching it has become a commonplace to recall the limitations inherent even in the most solemn formulations of the church. They can never hope to express fully and finally the experience of God that reached its unsurpassable climax in Jesus Christ. Rahner's warning has become classic: "The clearest formulations, the most sanctified formulas, the classic condensations of centuries-long work of the church in prayer, reflection and struggle concerning God's mysteries—all these derive their life from the fact that they are not an end but a beginning, not goals but means, truths which open their way to the ever greater Truth."[13] My point here is this: what we admit about the gap between experience and expression in the case of Christianity should encourage us to allow for something similar in other religions, instead of simply settling for their written teachings as the only place to look for the "seeds of the Word." In the words quoted at the start of this chapter from *Nostra Aetate*, we should look not only to the "precepts and doctrines" but also to the ways of "acting and living" in these other religions.

After attending to the task of sympathetic discernment, we turn finally to dialogue and cooperation with followers of other faiths. Like *Nostra Aetate*, we give most attention to Jews and Muslims.

---

13. K. Rahner, "Current Problems in Christology," *Theological Investigations* (London: Darton, Longman & Todd, 1961), 1:149.

7

Dialogue and Relations with Muslims and Jews

The interpretation and implementation—that is to say, reception—of Vatican II texts should and does press beyond the authorial intent of the original drafters to unfold meaning that these documents have also received from successive generations of readers and changing contexts. For instance, chains of meaning open up when we read the Declaration on the Relation of the Church to Non-Christian Religions in the context of post–Vatican II interfaith developments. The shortest of all the council's documents and the one that arguably had the most troubled passage to its final form, *Nostra Aetate* was given the lowest grade of authority as a "mere" declaration. But its subsequent reception has given this text a meaning and authority that go beyond what its authors imagined. In particular, the positive things said about Muslims (*NA* 3) and then Jews (*NA* 4–5) have taken on further meaning from subsequent history. This chapter reflects on those three articles of the declaration, in the light of what had come before and what would come later.

Nostra Aetate on Muslims

Since the Arab prophet Muhammad (d. 632) founded Islam, Vatican II was the first ecumenical council of the Catholic Church to offer some positive teaching on Muslims. The Second Council of Lyons (1274), meeting soon after the failure of the fifth and final (major) Crusade, described "the Saracens" as "blasphemous," "faithless," and "the impious enemies of the Christian name."[1] That was the only "teaching" on the followers of Islam to come from a general council before some brief remarks made by Vatican II in its 1964 Dogmatic Constitution on the Church, *Lumen Gentium*.

In article 107 of his first encyclical, *Ecclesiam Suam* (August 6, 1964), Pope Paul VI anticipated by a few months the new, positive teaching. He wrote of Muslims, "whom we do well to admire on account of those things that are true and commendable (*vera et probanda*) in their worship."[2] In considering "those who have not yet received the gospel" and "are ordered to the People of God for various reasons," *Lumen Gentium* highlighted the common ground it shared with Muslims: the divine "plan of salvation also embraces those who acknowledge the Creator, in the first place among whom are the Muslims. They profess to hold the faith of Abraham, and together with us they adore the one, merciful God, who will judge human beings on the last day" (*LG* 16).

While describing Muslims as those who "profess to hold the faith of Abraham" rather than simply state that Muslims hold the faith of Abraham, the council agreed that they "acknowledge the Creator" and, together with Christians, "adore the one, merciful God," and also share with Christians the hope of a general judgment "on the last day." A year later *Nostra Aetate* was to fill out this positive picture of Islam.

Lumen Gentium (implicitly) raised and left open the question: if Muslims "acknowledge the Creator" and, together with Christians, "adore the one, merciful God" who will come in judgment at the last day, how can Muslims do this without God having been revealed to them and their responding in faith?

---

1. N. P. Tanner (ed.), *Decrees of Ecumenical Councils* (London: Sheed & Ward, 1990), 1:309; hereafter Tanner. In the sixteenth century we find Martin Luther using such language of Muslims; see H.-M. Barth, *The Theology of Luther: A Critical Assessment* (Minneapolis: Fortress Press, 2013), 44–49.

2. *AAS* 56 (1964): 609–59, at 654.

How can this happen, moreover, unless in some sense God has made Islam a way of salvation for them? It is hard to escape the conclusion that at least the text of the constitution recognizes a certain revealing and saving efficacy in Islam. In some way the Muslim religion enjoys a specific role in mediating the knowledge of God and grace of God. Similar questions will emerge now when we come to *Nostra Aetate*.

The Declaration on the Relation of the Church to Non-Christian Religions devoted an entire article (*NA* 3) to the Muslims, first acknowledging major features in their doctrine of God: "They adore God, who is one, living and subsistent, merciful and almighty, the Creator of heaven and earth, who has spoken (*allocutum*) to human beings." This involves them in "submitting themselves wholeheartedly to the hidden decrees" of God, "just as Abraham submitted himself to God." The declaration added at once that "Islamic faith (*fides Islamica*) willingly refers itself" to Abraham—primarily, one presumes, to the faith of Abraham (and Sarah). The document remains silent, however, about the controversial issue of their historical descent from Abraham's son (Ishmael) claimed by Muslims.

While reluctant to state straight out that Muslims share the faith of Abraham and Sarah, *Nostra Aetate* clearly recognized how Muslims want to share that faith by "willingly" referring their faith to that of Abraham. Despite this reluctance, the article had already indicated how Islamic faith responded to divine revelation. It was because God had "spoken [in some kind of personal self-revelation] to human beings" and, specifically, to Muslims that they have come to faith in God as "one, living and subsistent, merciful and almighty, the Creator of heaven and earth." Hence they can truly "adore God," now revealed to them.[3] The divine self-revelation has made possible

---

3. To say that God had "spoken (*allocutum*) to human beings" evokes a traditional way of expressing divine revelation as *locutio Dei*, or God breaking silence and speaking to human beings. The verb *alloquor* corresponds to the noun *locutio*. Whether or not the drafters of *Nostra Aetate* consciously intended this meaning (*intentio auctoris*), the presence of

not only their worship of the true God but also their submission to God's decrees. To be sure, *Nostra Aetate* characterizes the "decrees" of God as "hidden." But, obviously, they cannot have remained totally and completely hidden. Otherwise how could Muslims have known what they should submit themselves to? God must have partially revealed the divine will to prompt such submission ("Islam" meaning "submission [to God]").

From the doctrine of God, the declaration moves its focus to Jesus: "They [the Muslims] do not acknowledge Jesus as God but venerate [him] as a prophet." They honor his virgin mother Mary," and "at times even devotedly invoke her." Since the Christian doctrine of God is trinitarian, it would be more accurate to speak of acknowledging or not acknowledging Jesus as "Son of God." The language about "honoring the virgin Mary" forms a slightly oblique way of stating that, along with Christians, Muslims believe that Jesus was virginally conceived through the power of God.[4]

Muslims sum up their faith by saying "there is no God but Allah and Muhammad is his prophet." But *Nostra Aetate* does not mention either the person of Muhammad or his prophetic character, or—for that matter—the Qur'an, *the* holy book of Islam containing the revelation said to have come through the archangel Gabriel to Muhammad.

Yet the declaration has indicated much common ground: (a) monotheistic faith in God revealed as the Creator of the universe (to which *Nostra Aetate* adds that Christians and Muslims alike "expect" the day when all human beings will be raised from the dead and divine judgment will be passed on them); and (b) the virginal conception of Jesus and his prophetic

---

the verb *alloquor* in their text expresses it (*intentio textus ipsius*); on an adequate theory for interpreting Vatican II texts that embraces authors, texts, and readers, see G. O'Collins, "Vatican II on 'Other' Ways of Salvation: A Valid Interpretation?," *Irish Theological Quarterly* 81 (2016): 152–70.

4. On the Muslim views of Jesus, see G. S. Reynolds, "The Islamic Christ," in Francesca A. Murphy and Troy A. Stefano (eds.), *The Oxford Handbook of Christology* (Oxford: Oxford University Press, 2015), 183–98.

identity. Here it is worth emphasizing that Christians, while believing in Jesus as more than a prophet, *also* understand his redemptive role in terms of a threefold office (*munus triplex*) as "priest, prophet, and king." The Second Vatican Council was to make Christ's office as priest, prophet, and king/shepherd a major theme by applying it to all the baptized, as well as to ordained priests and bishops.[5]

Finally, the declaration shows its esteem for the "moral life" of Muslims and the way they "worship God in prayer, alms-giving, and fasting." This is to mention three of the "Five Pillars of Islam," but leaves out two: (a) the profession of faith that includes the prophetic mission of Muhammad, and (b) the pilgrimage to Mecca, where Muhammad was born and received a first series of revelations. But *Nostra Aetate* never promised to provide a complete picture of Islam; it set itself to highlight some major features in the faith, practice, and worship of Muslims that establish common ground for dialogue and collaboration.

The article on Muslims (*NA* 3) concludes by referring to the "many" disagreements and open acts of hostility between Christians and Muslims that have occurred over the centuries. The council wants both sides to "forget the past" and "make a sincere effort at mutual understanding." Then, for the sake of all people, they will be able together to "protect and promote social justice, moral goods, peace and freedom." This conclusion, by recommending fresh efforts at dialogue and collabora-tion, matches what *Nostra Aetate* had encouraged when ending the previous article on world religions (which paid specific attention to Hinduism and Buddhism). Like others, I found the invitation to "forget the past" not particularly helpful. Sincere attempts at mutual forgiveness could lay a healthier and happier foundation for dialogue and practical collaboration between Christians and Muslims.

---

5. See G. O'Collins, *The Second Vatican Council: Message and Meaning* (Collegeville, MN: Liturgical Press, 2014), 1–24, at 19–20; see also 74–75.

Catholic–Muslim Relations after Vatican II

On May 6, 2001, less than four years before his death on April 2, 2005, Pope John Paul II visited the Umayyad Great Mosque in Damascus and became the first pope to enter and pray in a mosque since Muhammad founded Islam. His shoes were removed, and he put on white slippers before entering what had been the ancient Cathedral of John the Baptist and which contains the tomb of John the Baptist, known and honored as Yahya in the Muslim tradition. Far from forgetting the past, the pope recalled "the misuse of religion itself to promote or justify hatred or violence." On the basis of a common faith in God the Creator, he added: "Violence destroys the image of the Creator in his creatures and should never be considered as the fruit of religious conviction." He prayed that "Muslim and Christian religious leaders and teachers will present our two great religious communities as communities in respectful dialogue, never more as communities in conflict." Furthermore, "at the start of the third millennium," he hoped that Muslims and Christians would "find a new way of presenting our two religions not in opposition but in partnership for the good of the human family."[6]

This outreach to Muslims belonged to John Paul II's vision of the deep unity of those who, despite divisions, find in spiritual values and religious faith a profound answer to the basic questions of the human heart. The Declaration on the Relationship of the Church to Non-Christian Religions had listed seven questions that unavoidably touch human hearts and minds:

> What is the human being? What is the meaning and purpose of our life? What is good [behavior] and what is sin? What is the origin of sufferings and what is their purpose? What is the way to obtain happiness? What

---

6. *Origins* 31/1 (May 17, 2001): 13–14, at 14; see Christian W. Troll, "John Paul II and Islam," in G. O'Collins and M. A. Hayes (eds.), *The Legacy of John Paul II* (London: Burns & Oates, 2008), 203–27.

is death, judgment, and final accounting after death? What, finally, is that ultimate and ineffable mystery that enfolds our existence, from which we take our origin and toward which we move (*NA* 1)?

These questions, which enjoy a long and wide heritage in human cultures and religions, held together John Paul's openness to living faiths in our world.[7]

The text of *Nostra Aetate* and, in particular, what it taught about Muslims have taken on further meaning in the post-1965 history of the declaration's interpretation and implementation, when theological ideals encountered religious and political realities and Catholics engaged with religious "others." That history includes the teaching of popes and their "gestures" (e.g. the meeting in the Vatican Gardens of Pope Francis on June 9, 2014, with Shimon Peres, the Israeli president, and Mahmoud Abbas, the Palestinian president); the work of the Pontifical Council for Interreligious Dialogue (and numerous similar bodies around the world); teaching programs developed by Gabriel Said Reynolds at the University of Notre Dame, Indiana, and similar academic initiatives promoted elsewhere.

Apropos of John Paul II and the Muslims, some writers have highlighted what the pope said about the difference between Christianity and Islam in the course of the 1994 interview with Vittorio Messori. Reading the Bible and comparing it with the Qur'an, he detected a "process by which it [the Qur'an] completely reduces the Divine Revelation."[8] But, as Christian

---

7. See Aleksander Mazur, *L'insegnamento di Giovanni Paolo II sulle altre religioni* (Rome: Gregorian University Press, 2004). This book contains references to all that John Paul II said about Islam (92–100, 188–92). Unlike other authors, Mazur cites and evaluates what the pope said when addressing bishops from Muslim countries and when addressing various audiences on his visits to Muslim countries. Mazur's full bibliography seems to omit only one relevant item, John Paul II's 1986 Christmas address to the Roman Curia.

8. John Paul II, *Crossing the Threshold of Hope* (London: Jonathan Cape, 1994), 92.

Troll has written, "One could query John Paul's statement that in Islam *all* of God's self-revelation has been set aside." Troll points out that the Qur'an, in "naming God in manifold ways, describing him, for example, as merciful, clement and all-knowing, does in effect truly reveal qualities of God's nature in the sense of God revealing in these koranic phrases aspects of Himself which mere reason would not be able to reach." Troll judges that the late pope seemed to have lacked "a sufficiently differentiated knowledge of Islam, in consequence of which he arrived at a too undifferentiated assessment" of "the different Muslim images of God."[9] In any case, *Crossing the Threshold of Hope* expresses the personal opinions of John Paul II, not his magisterial teaching as Bishop of Rome.

Those who play up these personal views of John Paul II sometimes play down or simply ignore what he said as pope in Casablanca on August 19, 1985, which should be ranked as official, or "magisterial," teaching, even if obviously not at the highest level. At the invitation of King Hassan II of Morocco, he spoke as Bishop of Rome and head of the Catholic Church to a crowd of over one hundred thousand young Muslims about the religious and moral values common to Christian and Muslim faith.[10] "We have many things in common as believers," he told the young Muslims, and added at once: "Abraham is the model for us all of faith in God." This common faith responds to the divine revelation that reaches both groups: "God reveals himself as the one who pardons and gives mercy. So our love and adoration go out to him. For his benefits and his mercy we give him thanks at all times and everywhere." John Paul II ended by associating Christian with Muslim faith, by recalling "the Three Good Names [Unknowable, Creator, Revealer] our religious traditions attribute to" God, and by invoking God, the final judge of all, "the Author of justice and

---

9. Troll, "John Paul II and Islam," 207, 208.

10. *AAS* 78 (1986): 95–104; English trans. from original French, G. O'Collins, D. Kendall, and J. LaBelle (eds.), *John Paul II: A Reader* (Mahwah, NJ: Paulist Press, 2007), 148–58.

peace," in a moving prayer in which Muslims could join.[11] Even
more clearly than *Nostra Aetate*, the pope recognized that, for
Muslims also, God's self-revelation has initiated true faith that
expresses itself in prayer, love, adoration, and thanksgiving.

The post–Vatican II engagement of Catholics (and other
Christians), either officially or unofficially, with Muslims has
opened up meanings in the text of *Nostra Aetate*. The continu-
ing volumes of *Christian Muslim Relations: A Bibliographical
History* (Leiden: Brill) and the bibliographical surveys (2003–)
by Massimo Faggioli (in the journal *Cristianesimo nella storia*)
of Vatican II documents direct researchers to relevant material in the ongoing interpretation and implementation of the
Declaration on the Relation of the Church to Non-Christian
Religions. Such help is also forthcoming from various authors
or editors listed in the bibliography for this book: for instance,
Mahmut Aydin, James Heft, Risto Jutto, and Byron Sherwin
(with Harold Kasimow). Let me cite one contributor.

In "The Qur'an and the Doctrine of Private Revelation,"[12]
Anna Bonta Moreland presents her ongoing work in exploring whether Catholics and other Christians might consider
Muhammad to have received what have been called "private
revelations" and might reconsider what comprises prophecy.[13]
In the course of her article, she retrieves from Yves Congar,
the leading theologian at Vatican II who had a hand in draft-
ing eight of the sixteen documents, a fascinating, if individ-
ualistic, observation found in a 1937 article in *Vie spirituelle*:
"Private revelations are commonly understood as those revelations in which a soul, *be it Christian or not*, is the subject of

---

11. *John Paul II: A Reader,* 149, 150, 157.
12. Anna Bonta Moreland, "The Qur'an and the Doctrine of Private Revelstion: A Theological Proposal," *Theological Studies* 76 (2015):
531–49.
13. On this see Christian Troll, "Muhammad—Prophet for Christians
also?," in O'Collins and Hayes, *The Legacy of John Paul II*, 252–68. He sets
out his reasons for not calling Muhammad a prophet but rather "an out-
standing political and religious founder-figure, who has led many people
to God" (267).

God on a personal or private level, and not as an initiator or a doctor of the universal religion in which God works the salvation of humanity."[14] In other words, the one who authentically receives such a divine message need not be a Christian. She also retrieves a very relevant suggestion from an article by Daniel Madigan, "*Nostra Aetate* and the Questions It Chose to Leave Open."[15] In the light of the declaration abstaining from passing judgments about religions taken as a whole, he urged the case for asking particular questions:

> Instead of asking "Is this religion a structure or vehicle or way of salvation?," should we not ask: "Are there elements in this religion that God appears to be using to save people?" Thus there is no single, a priori answer to the question of how salvific other religions are. We can only make a posteriori judgment, based on an observation of the fruits of the Spirit and the distinguishing marks of the Kingdom in the followers of that particular religion. Such an a posteriori judgment cannot or need not be made about the whole religion, but rather about individual elements.[16]

Moreland draws the conclusion: "particular passages in the Qur'an could be explored without having to make any claims about the book as a whole."[17]

Lumen Gentium on Jews:
The Background and the Text

For many centuries the persecution of Jews disfigured horribly the story of many Christian communities. Encouraged by

---

14. Moreland, "The Qur'an and the Doctrine of Private Revelation," 544–45; her trans. and emphasis.

15. Daniel Madigan, "*Nostra Aetate* and the Questions It Chose to Leave Open," *Gregorianum* 87 (2006): 781–96.

16. Ibid., 787–88.

17. Moreland, "The Qur'an and the Doctrine of Private Revelation," 548.

wrong-headed interpretations of certain NT texts (e.g. Matt. 27:4–5; 1 Thess. 2:14–16), from the fourth century some Christian writers indulged in anti-Jewish polemics. Thus St. John Chrysostom (d. 407), while still a presbyter in Antioch and not yet Patriarch of Constantinople, preached eight sermons aimed at stopping Christians from attending synagogues and following Jewish practices. His sharp rhetoric cast a long shadow on Christian–Jewish relations. Collectively accused of being "Christ-killers" and deicides ("God-killers"), Jews suffered violent attacks from the eleventh century on; in some cases whole communities were wiped out.

Saint Bernard of Clairvaux raised his voice in protest against such crimes, addressing a notorious anti-Semite, the monk Raoul, in the language John 8:44 used of the devil: "I suppose that it is enough for you to be as your master. He was a murderer from the beginning, a liar, and the father of lies" (*Letter* 365). Bernard saw faith as always a matter of persuasion and never of compulsion, and so rejected forced conversion of Jews or others. Nevertheless, dreadful legends about Jews murdering children, poisoning water supplies, and desecrating the Eucharist fostered killings and expulsions. Jewish people were driven out of England (1290), France (1394), Spain (1492), and Portugal (1496). The Fourth Lateran Council had helped to trigger evil results. Its 1215 decree on Jews excluded them from public office and required them (and "Saracens," that is to say, Muslims) to be distinguished from Christians in their dress.[18]

In presenting the necessity of the church for salvation, the Council of Florence in 1442 taught that "no one remaining outside the Church, not only pagans but also Jews, heretics and schismatics, can become partakers of eternal life, but they will go to the eternal fire prepared for the devil and his angels [Matt. 25:41], unless before the end of their lives they are joined to it [the church]" (ND 1005, DzH 1351).[19] This

---

18. Tanner, 1:266–67.

19. Ibid., 1:578. The Council of Florence went so far in opposing Jewish religious observances that it warned Christians who practice circum-

frightening warning went out against others but only as "general" categories (pagans, heretics, and schismatics); it specified Jews as being in such dire peril. Yet fifty years later, when in 1492 Ferdinand and Isabella expelled Jews from Spain, Pope Alexander VI welcomed them to the papal states—a decision recalled with gratitude by the Jews of Rome on the occasion of Pope John Paul II visiting their Great Synagogue (April 13, 1986).

In most European countries, the nineteenth century brought an emancipation of Jews that made possible, for instance, Benjamin Disraeli becoming British prime minister (1868 and 1874–80). Nevertheless, Pope Pius IX reinstated in Rome a closed ghetto for Jews and introduced anti-Jewish legislation. The fall of the papal states in 1870 put an end to that. Yet pogroms or massacres of Jews continued to happen in Russia; and across Europe and elsewhere Catholic leaders often did little to counteract the poisonous influence of anti-Semitism. Pope Pius XI, however, reacted to Adolf Hitler's persecution of Jews by declaring in the encyclical *Mit brennender Sorge* (1937) that it is impossible for a Christian to accept anti-Semitism, because "through Christ and in Christ we are of Abraham's spiritual stock. Spiritually we are Semites."[20]

During the Second World War (1939–45), when fifty-five million people were killed or starved to death, one act of willful murder stands out: The Shoah. Hitler and his collaborators systematically eliminated nearly six million Jews, one million of them children. After Rolf Hochhuth attacked Pius XII (pope 1939–58) in a play, *The Deputy: A Christian Tragedy* (1964),[21] it became popular to accuse Pius XII of failure to challenge the Nazis publicly over their dreadful murder of Jews. The grounds for attack have often shifted over the years: from "He was

---

cision that, "whether one puts one's hope in it or not, it cannot in any way be observed without loss of eternal salvation" (ND 1003; DzH 1348).

20. Pius XI, *Documentation Catholique* 39 (1938): col. 1460, 19.

21. Rolf Hochhuth, *The Deputy: A Christian Tragedy* (New York: Grove Press, 1964).

indifferent to Jewish suffering in the Holocaust" (Hochhuth) to "He was not as concerned about Nazi efforts to eliminate Jews as he should have been."[22] In contrast, numerous writers have defended Pius XII for all that he did to save Jews. At one point during the German occupation of Rome (September 1943 to June 1944), the SS arrested 1,007 Roman Jews and sent them to Auschwitz. Fifteen survived. During the same period, 477 Jews were hidden in Vatican City itself, and 4,238 were given sanctuary in Rome's monasteries and convents. But should Pius XII have publicly denounced the persecution of Jews, and specifically their deportation to Auschwitz?[23]

In a 1986 study Owen Chadwick showed how Pius XII was party to a plot against Hitler in the winter of 1939/40. Recently Mark Riebling has used extensive German sources to document how the pope continued this clandestine opposition to Nazi crimes, and through his representatives provided steady encouragement to the German resistance and the actions they took to kill Hitler and end the war.[24] A Jewish professor of history and political science, David G. Dalin, has answered the case against Pius XII brought by Cornwell and others.[25] An indispensable source is provided by the eleven volumes of documents from the Vatican archives that cover the period of the Second World War (published by Pierre Blet and his fellow historians up to 1981). But scholars still wait for the full opening of the Vatican archives. In any case, a "what if" question can probably never be answered by any documents. If Pius XII had issued a public and quite explicit condemnation of the Nazi

---

22. John Cornwell, *Hitler's Pope: The Secret History of Pius XII* (New York: Viking Press, 1999).

23. See Owen Chadwick, *Britain and the Vatican during the Second World War* (Cambridge: Cambridge University Press, 1986), 288–89; Susan Zuccotti, *Under His Very Windows: The Vatican and the Holocaust in Italy* (New Haven, CT: Yale University Press, 2000), 181–86, 200.

24. M. Riebling, *Church of Spies: The Pope's Secret War Against Hitler* (London: Scribe, 2015).

25. D. G. Dalin, *The Myth of Hitler's Pope* (Washington, DC: Regnery, 2005).

murder of Jews, would the Nazis have reacted as they did to a condemnation by the Dutch bishops when they deported forty thousand Jews to extermination camps?[26]

It was against this ancient and more recent background that St. John XXIII (pope 1958–63), Cardinal Augustin Bea (1881–1968), and others led the Second Vatican Council into some positive teaching on Jews and their relationship with Christians. In 1959 the pope made Bea a cardinal and in 1960 the first president of the Secretariat for the Promotion of the Unity of Christians (later the Pontifical Council for Promoting Unity), a post that he held until his death and through which he developed relations not only with other Christians but also with the Jewish people. He was a decisive force in securing the council's repudiation of anti-Semitism in *Nostra Aetate*. But we should recall the teaching that came a year earlier from *Lumen Gentium*.

The key response of *Lumen Gentium* about understanding the religious "others" in the light of Christian faith comes in two articles (16 and 17). An earlier article (*LG* 13) frames the scope of what will be said. Holding in faith that, through Christ's redeeming work, "all human beings are called" to the new People of God, the council reflects on how, "in different ways," they "belong" (*pertinent*) or "are ordered" (*ordinantur*) to catholic unity.

In considering how "those who have not yet received the gospel" are "ordered" to the new People of God, the document, before moving to Muslims, selected some of the privileges listed by Romans 9:4–5 that speak of "the people to whom the covenants and promises were given and from whom Christ was born according to the flesh (see Rom. 9:4–5)." Then it aligned itself again with Paul by stating that "According to the [divine] election, they [the Jews] are a people most dear [to God] on account of their fathers, for God does not take back his gifts and calling (see Rom. 11:28–29)." This was the first time in the

---

26. Riebling, *Church of Spies*, 131–33.

history of Catholic Christianity that an ecumenical council had spoken well of the Jews.

Before Vatican II, no council had ever cited Romans 9:4–5 and 11:28–29. The council found its scriptural warrant in Paul's texts about God's irrevocable election of Israel.[27] In the longer treatment of the Jewish people that came a year later in *Nostra Aetate*, the council once again quoted Romans 9:4–5 (*NA* 4), and in a reference to Romans 11:28–29 recalled the use of that verse in *Lumen Gentium* (*NA* 4 n. 11). A sea change in attitudes toward Jews involved Vatican II in appealing to two passages from Paul, which no previous council had ever invoked. Attention to previously neglected scriptural witness helped inspire new teaching.

We find other such examples of developments in teaching being inspired and expressed by long-ignored biblical testimony. No ecumenical council had, for instance, appealed to Genesis 1:26–27 and what it said about human beings "created in the image and likeness of God" until the promulgation of *Nostra Aetate* in late 1965. This declaration clearly echoed, even if it did not explicitly cite, the Genesis doctrine about all people being "created in the image of God," and drew a practical conclusion: that there is no basis for any discrimination that offends against or curtails "human dignity and the rights that flow from it" (*NA* 5). "Human Dignity" would become the title of the Declaration on Religious Liberty promulgated a few weeks later, on December 7, 1965. *Gaudium et Spes*, promulgated on the same day, would insist "on the extraordinary dignity of the human person" and the basic rights that flow from that dignity (*GS* 26; see *GS* 29). In the context of *Nostra Aetate*, insistence on "human dignity and the rights that flow from it"

---

27. Romans 9:4–5 appeared in what would become the text of *LG*, thanks to the schema elaborated by Gérard Philips that, from February 1963, became the basis for a revised draft. After emendations were received, Romans 11:28–29 entered the text in 1964. See G. Alberigo and F. Magistretti, *Constitutionis Dogmaticae Lumen Gentium Synopsis Historica* (Bologna: Institute for Religious Sciences, 1975), 71.

evoked the tragic way in which that dignity and those rights had been flouted by centuries of anti-Semitism and, even more horribly, by the Holocaust.

Nostra Aetate on Jews

Mainly because of differences over what should be said about the relationship between Christians and Jews, the final text of *Nostra Aetate* had a troubled history as it moved toward the document finally approved in late 1965. Its first version (actually its second draft) came before the council in November 1964 as Chapter 4 ("On the Relationship of Catholics to Non-Christians and especially to Jews") in a "schema" for the Decree on Ecumenism (*Unitatis Redintegratio*).[28] A new draft of this chapter was then moved to being an appendix in the same decree and was renamed as "A Further Declaration on Jews and Non-Christians." It was then proposed as an appendix to *Lumen Gentium*, with the title "On the Relation of the Church to Non-Christian Religions." Finally, it kept the same title but became a self-standing document. A debate in November 1964 opened the way for a final, emended form voted on and approved during the council's fourth and closing session.[29]

Where *Lumen Gentium* dedicates only one sentence to Jews and appeals only to Paul's Letter to the Romans, *Nostra Aetate*

---

28. In January 1964, Pope Paul VI, by making a pilgrimage to the Holy Land, had helped to prepare a positive outcome to the conciliar debate on relationship with the Jews.

29. See G. Miccioli, "Two Sensitive Issues: Religious Freedom and the Jews," in G. Alberigo and J. A. Komonchak (eds.), *History of Vatican II* (Maryknoll, NY: Orbis Books, 2003), 4:135–93; M. Velati, "Completing the Conciliar Agenda," *History of Vatican II*, 5:185–273, at 211–31; J. M. Oesterreicher, "Declaration on the Relationship of the Church to Non-Christian Religions," in H. Vorgrimler (ed.), *Commentary on the Documents of Vatican II* (London: Burns & Oates, 1969), 3:1–136; R. A. Siebenrock, "Theologischer Kommentar zur Erklärung über die Haltung der Kirche zu den nichtchristlichen Religionen *Nostra Aetate*," in P. Hünermann and B. J Hilberath (eds.), *Herders Theologischer Kommentar zum Zweiten Vatikanischen Konzil* (Freiburg: Herder, 2005), 3:591–693.

presented the Catholic–Jewish relationship in an entire article (the longest in the whole document) and appealed to a spread of OT and NT texts (*NA* 4). The article began by summarizing elements in God's plan that linked the church with the Jewish people, In general, all the church's faithful are sons and daughters of our father in faith, Abraham, and "included in his call." Thus "the church's faith and election" originated in the patriarchs, Moses, and the prophets. In particular, the salvation of the church was "prefigured in the exodus of God's chosen people from the land of bondage" and the covenant God established with them at Sinai. The church also received from them "the revelation of the Old Testament"—or, in other words, the inspired scriptures, which recorded and applied the revealing words and deeds of God and which, among other things, provided the church with its central prayer book, the Psalms. *Nostra Aetate* also recalls those Jews who brought the church into existence: Christ himself, "the son of Mary," the apostles ("the pillars on which the church stands"), and many of the early disciples who proclaimed the good news to the world.

To this picture of the church's Jewish origins one might add further items: for instance, the Jewish heritage that helped fashion the basic sacraments of baptism and the Eucharist, as well as the extensive reflection on the human condition in all its weaknesses and possibilities that no adequate Christian anthropology should ever neglect. In fact, the Jewish heritage should shape Christian thinking about the church, creation, and divine providence, the gift of grace to sinful human beings, their sacramental life and their moral behavior (e.g. the Ten Commandments)—not to mention providing the central language for Christology and the doctrine of the Trinity (God the Father, the Son/Word/Wisdom, and the Spirit of God).

Lumen Gentium had turned to the Pauline letters to expound the church's relationship with the Jewish people. *Nostra Aetate* follows suit, highlighting the image in Romans 11 of the Gentiles being "the wild olive branches grafted into the good olive tree," and then moving to Ephesians and what it says about

"Christ as our peace who through his cross reconciled Jews and Gentiles and made them one in himself" (Eph. 2:14–16). Even if many Jews did not accept the gospel, the Jews, as Paul teaches in Romans, "remain very dear to God," who "does not take back the gifts he bestowed or the choice he made."

Facing squarely the traditional accusation of collective guilt brought against Jews, *Nostra Aetate* insists that "not all Jews at that time nor Jews today can be charged with crimes committed during the passion" of Christ. The council emphasizes that it was "because of the sins of all people" (one thinks of "all have sinned" in Rom. 3:23) and for the salvation of all that Christ "out of infinite love" underwent death. It is as the sign of God's universal love and the source of all grace" that the cross should be proclaimed. "Jews should not be spoken of as rejected or cursed" by God. Remembering its "common heritage with the Jews," the church, represented by the bishops at Vatican II, "deplores (*reprobat*) all hatreds, persecutions, displays of anti-Semitism at any time or from any source leveled against the Jews."

Sadly this judgment came only after many centuries of Jewish suffering, but, thankfully, even if it did not explicitly mention the Holocaust, it did finally come. It was followed up in the final article of *Nostra Aetate* with a more general censure: "The church deplores (*reprobat*), as foreign to the mind of Christ, any discrimination against people or any harassment of them on the basis of their race, color, condition in life, or religion" (*NA* 5).

In 1960, two years before he opened the sessions of Vatican II, John XXIII had removed from the Good Friday prayers a traditional phrase about "the perfidious Jews." Now, two years after his death, the council had realized his desire to condemn anti-Semitism and recognize the heritage Christians share with Jews. Many years earlier, he had saved around 24,000 Jews when he was apostolic delegate to Turkey and Greece (1934–44).[30]

---

30. See Thomas Cahill, *Pope John XXIII* (London: Phoenix, 2003), 153–56.

Catholic–Jewish Relations after Vatican II

The headlines of post–Vatican II Catholic engagement with Jews from 1965 to date are found (1) in some Roman documents and (2) in what popes have done and said. The small print, which is immense, includes all kinds of collaboration and fraternal dialogue that have taken place around the world. To cite one personal example, with my fellow organizers (Stephen Davis and Daniel Kendall), I made sure that at least one Jewish scholar (Alan Segal) participated in the four "summits" we organized for an ecumenical team of Christians in Yonkers (New York): on the resurrection (1996), the Trinity (1998), the incarnation (2000), and redemption (2003); Segal contributed a chapter to the first three volumes we produced. Along with Segal, a second Jewish scholar (Peter Ochs) attended the "summit" of 2003, and his chapter appeared in the volume published subsequently.[31] My deep conviction is that Jewish scholars keep Christian scholars honest; it is from Jewish faith that Christian faith developed and the church emerged. It is at their peril that Christians ignore the Jewish matrix of their religion.

Roman Documents

In October 1974, Paul VI set right a misunderstanding that *Nostra Aetate* could cause.

As a Declaration on the Relation of the Church to Non-Christian Religions, the document seemed to imply that Judaism, like Hinduism and Buddhism, ranked as a "non-Christian" religion. The pope instituted the Commission for Religious Relations with the Jews and joined this special commission to (what was still called then) the Secretariat for Promoting Christian Unity.

---

31. Oxford University Press published the four volumes: *Resurrection* (1997), *The Trinity* (1999), *The Incarnation* (2002), and *The Redemption* (2004).

The commission lost no time in issuing in December 1974 "Guidelines on Religious Relations with the Jews."[32] Among other things, this document, even more clearly than *Nostra Aetate*, recalled (in its introduction) "the persecution and massacre of Jews which took place in Europe just before and during the Second World War." Far more was to be said about the Shoah and the duty to remember it, when, in view of the coming millennium, the same commission published *We Remember: A Reflection on the Shoah* in 1998. In the Jubilee Year of 2000 this document found its liturgical counterpart at the Mass celebrated in St. Peter's Basilica on the First Sunday of Lent. The bidding prayers included a confession of guilt and prayer for forgiveness over the terrible failure of Christians who did not speak up for the Jews and protect them.

In November 2005, the Pontifical Biblical Commission published "The Jewish People and Their Sacred Scriptures in the Christian Bible." The final section of this remarkable document states: "the Jewish sacred Scriptures constitute an essential part of the Christian Bible . . . without the Old Testament, the New Testament would be an incomprehensible book, a plant deprived of its roots and destined to dry up and wither" (art. 84).

Finally, in 2015 the Commission for Religious Relations with the Jews published "The Gifts and Calling of God Are Irrevocable." The document stressed more than ever the Jewish origins of Christianity and, in particular, the identity of Jesus as a faithful Jew. On the practical level, it stated: "The Catholic Church neither conducts nor supports any specific institutional mission work directed toward Jews." The title of this document recalled what John Paul II had said in 1988 (see below). To hold that God's covenant with the Jews had never been revoked obviously leaves one with the question: Why then should Jews be asked to convert to Christianity?

---

32. In 1985, the commission produced "Notes on the Correct Way to present the Jews and Judaism in Preaching and Catechesis in the Roman Catholic Church."

Without wanting the Catholic–Jewish dialogue to be hijacked by politics, let me recall that in 1993 the Vatican and Israel established diplomatic relations, and that in 2015 the Vatican signed a treaty formally recognizing the State of Palestine.

Vatican II and its aftermath have brought a positive revolution in Catholic–Jewish relations. But, on the one hand, this revolution still has to reach many Catholic parishes and other organizations. On the other hand, in the State of Israel school courses in the history of Christianity move through the Crusades and the Spanish Inquisition, and stop with the Holocaust. At an international conference on interfaith dialogue held at Australian Catholic University in Melbourne (May 26–29, 2014), Deborah Weissman spoke to the question, "Has there been a Jewish Response to *Nostra Aetate*?" She regretted that a knowledge of what Vatican II taught in *Nostra Aetate* had failed to reach many of her fellow Jews.

Papal Words and Deeds

We have already seen a little of the impact of papal words and "gestures" on Catholic–Muslim relations in the aftermath of Vatican II. As regards the Catholic–Jewish relations, Paul VI, John Paul II, Benedict XVI, and now Francis have played major roles, with John Paul II towering above the other three popes.[33]

Less than a year after being elected pope, in June 1979, John Paul II made a pilgrimage to Auschwitz; as a young man he had experienced firsthand the hideous tragedy of the Shoah. In the first year of his pontificate Benedict XVI would also visit Auschwitz and speak of those who by "destroying Israel" showed how they "wanted to tear up the taproot of the Christian faith."[34] On April 13, 1986, John Paul II did something no Bishop of Rome had ever done or, at least, had never done

---

33. See Gregory Glazov, "Jewish Suffering and Christology in Pauline and Recent Papal Thought," in Murphy and Stefano, *Oxford Handbook of Christology*, 39–54; and Margaret Shepherd, "John Paul II and Catholic-Jewish Dialogue," in O'Collins and Hayes, *Legacy of John Paul II*, 228–51.

34. See Glazov, "Jewish Suffering and Christology," 41.

since the time of early Christianity: he visited a synagogue: namely, the Great Synagogue in Rome, situated in the area of the former ghetto. There he addressed the Jewish congregation: "You are our elder brothers."

As I write this chapter, Pope Francis has also just visited the Roman synagogue (January 16, 2016). Stressing the "Jewish roots of Christianity," he summed up the results of Vatican II: "From enemies and strangers we have become sisters and brothers . . . 'Yes' to the rediscovery of the Jewish roots of Christianity. 'No' to any form of anti-Semitism." In his apostolic exhortation of November 2013, Pope Francis had already declared: "As Christians, we cannot consider Judaism as a foreign religion . . . dialogue and friendship with the children of Israel are part of the life of Jesus' disciples." He explained why Christians should cherish the Jewish people in a special way: "Their covenant with God has never been revoked" (247–48). Back on November 17, 1980, John Paul II, when speaking to representatives of the Jewish community in Mainz, had affirmed quite clearly the irrevocable nature of the covenant with God's people[35]—something left slightly implicit in the teaching of *Lumen Gentium* and *Nostra Aetate* (see above).

The teaching of *Nostra Aetate* opened the door for a reconciliation with the Jewish people that was practiced, at times dramatically, during the pontificate of John Paul II. In 1994 he hosted a Holocaust-memorial concert in the Vatican, and sat with the chief rabbi of Rome, who had brought with him his congregation. The concert was part of the pope's personal mission to keep alive the memory of the Holocaust. His visit to Israel (March 2000) was an even more important landmark in renewed relations with the Jewish people.[36] In May 2014, Pope Francis made his pilgrimage to the Holy Land.

---

35. *AAS* 73 (1981): 78–82, at 80.
36. See Shepherd, "John Paul II," 239–43.

Conclusion

A Christology of religions, as the final chapter has attempted to show, should look beyond ways of thinking and teaching. It includes the practice of living a theology of religions centered on Jesus Christ, a practice that interprets and implements what Vatican II enunciated, above all, in *Nostra Aetate*. In recent years we have seen the practice of interfaith encounter exemplified strikingly by John Paul II and Pope Francis. Rather than capitulating to a fear, which sees "the other" as a threat and an enemy, Pope Francis in an address to the diplomatic corps (January 11, 2016) firmly endorsed the "culture of encounter." Right from the start of his pontificate he has practiced such a culture. Within weeks of his election, he celebrated the liturgy of Holy Thursday in a prison for young offenders and washed the feet of a young Muslim woman—a gesture that may do more for Catholic–Muslim relations than thousands of words.

8

Epilogue

In conclusion, what might I claim that this book has achieved? At least seven themes establish the new ground broken by this book: Christology of religions as the preferred name for this theological discipline; the relevance of the theology of the cross; Christ's high priesthood as central to the argument; his universal, active presence, along with that of the Holy Spirit; the efficacy of prayer for "others" inspired by love and joined with Christ's own intercession; Hebrews as a source for understanding the faith of "other" suffering human beings; and four criteria for identifying experiences that hint at the active presence of the risen Christ and the Holy Spirit.

Some scholars have noted a current stalemate in the debates between those concerned with the theology of religions. My hope is that the introduction of my seven themes may help to break this stalemate and breathe new life into thinking about the religious "others," learning from them, and collaborating with them on projects for the good of the human family—not least the essential project of peace.

For more than a century Christians have kept the Week of Prayer for Christian Unity. The United Nations observes the World Interfaith Harmony Week (February 1–7). A Week of Prayer for Interfaith Unity seems long overdue.

Selected Bibliography

Alangaram, A. *Christ of the Asian Peoples: Towards an Asian Contextual Christology.* 2nd ed. Bangalore: Asian Trading Corporation, 2001.

Alberigo, Giuseppe, and Joseph A. Komonchak, eds. *History of Vatican II,* 5 vols. Maryknoll, NY: Orbis Books, 1995–2006.

Aydin, Mahmut. *Modern Western Christian Theological Understandings of Muslims since the Second Vatican Council.* Washington, DC: Council for Research in Values and Philosophy, 2002.

Becker, Karl-Josef, and Ilaria Morali, eds. *Catholic Engagement with World Religions: A Comprehensive Study.* Maryknoll, NY: Orbis Books, 2010.

Bevershuis, Joel, ed. *Sourcebook of the World's Religions: An Interfaith Guide to Religion and Spirituality.* Novato, CA: New World Library, 2000.

Bowman, Glenn, ed. *Sharing the Sacred.* Oxford: Berghahn Books, 2012.

Burrows, William R. *Jacques Dupuis Faces the Inquisition: Two Essays by Jacques Dupuis on* Dominus Iesus *and the Roman Investigation of His Work.* Eugene, OR: Pickwick Publications, 2012.

Cohen, Charles L., Paul F. Knitter, and Ulrich Rosenhagen, eds. *The Future of Interreligious Dialogue: A Multireligious Conversation on* Nostra Aetate. Maryknoll, NY: Orbis Books, 2017.

Connelly, John. *From Enemy to Brother: The Revolution in Catholic Teaching on the Jews, 1933–65.* Cambridge, MA: Harvard University Press, 2012.

Cornille, Catherine. *The Im-possibility of Interreligious Dialogue.* New York: Crossroad, 2008.

———. "Soteriological Agnosticism and the Future of Catholic Theology of Interreligious Dialogue." In *The Past, Present, and Future of Theologies of Interreligious Dialogue,* 201–15. Edited by T. Merrigan and J. Friday. Oxford: Oxford University Press, 2017.

————, ed. *The Wiley-Blackwell Companion to Interreligious Dialogue.* Chichester, UK: Wiley, 2013.

Clooney, Francis X. *Comparative Theology: Deep Learning across Religious Borders.* Malden, MA: Wiley-Blackwell, 2010.

————. *His Hiding Place Is Darkness: A Hindu-Christian Theopoetics of Divine Absence.* Stanford, CA: Stanford University Press, 2014.

Cunningham, Philip A. et al., eds. *The Catholic Church and the Jewish People: Recent Reflections from Rome.* New York: Fordham University Press, 2007.

Cunningham, Philip A., ed. *Christ Jesus and the Jewish People Today: New Explorations of Theological Relationship.* Grand Rapids, MI: Eerdmans, 2011.

D'Costa, Gavin. *Theology and Religious Pluralism: The Challenge of Other Religions.* Oxford: Blackwell, 1986.

————. *The Meeting of Religions and the Trinity.* Maryknoll, NY: Orbis Books, 2000.

Di Noia, Joseph. *The Diversity of Religions: A Christian Perspective.* Washington, DC: Catholic University of America Press, 1992.

Dupuis, Jacques. *Toward a Christian Theology of Religious Pluralism.* Maryknoll, NY: Orbis Books, 1997.

————. *Christianity and the Religions: From Confrontation to Dialogue.* Maryknoll, NY: Orbis Books, 2002.

Ellis, Kalil C., ed. *Vatican, Islam, and the Middle East.* Syracuse, NY: Syracuse University Press, 1987.

Gethin, Rupert. *The Foundations of Buddhism.* Oxford: Oxford University Press, 1998.

Goshen-Gottstein, Alon, ed. *Friendship across Religions: Theological Perspectives on Interreligious Friendship.* Lanham, MD: Lexington, 2015.

Griffith, Sidney H. *The Church in the Shadow of the Mosque: Christians and Muslims in the World of Islam.* Princeton, NJ: Princeton University Press, 2008.

Heft, James, ed. *Catholicism and Interreligious Dialogue.* New York: Oxford University Press, 2011.

Hick, John, and Paul Knitter. *The Myth of Christian Uniqueness: Toward a Pluralistic Theology of Religion.* Maryknoll, NY: Orbis Books, 1987.

Hünermann, Peter, and Bernd-Jochen Hilberath, eds. *Herders Theologischer Kommentar zum Zweiten Vatikanischen Konzil,* 5 vols. Freiburg: Herder, 2004–2006.

Ipgrave, Michael, ed. *Bearing the Word: Prophecy in Biblical Qur'anic Perspective.* London: Church House, 2005.

Jutto, Risto. *Trinity in Unity in Christian–Muslim Relations: The Work of the Pontifical Council for Interreligious Dialogue.* Leiden: Brill, 2007.

Kendall, Daniel, and Gerald O'Collins. *In Many and Diverse Ways: In Honor of Jacques Dupuis.* Maryknoll, NY: Orbis Books, 2003.

Keown, Damien. *Buddhism: A Very Short Introduction.* Oxford: Oxford University Press, 1996.

Knott, Kim. *Hinduism: A Very Short Introduction.* Oxford: Oxford University Press, 2000.

Lamptey, Jerusha Tanner. *Never Wholly Other: A Muslima Theology of Religious Pluralism.* New York: Oxford University Press, 2014.

Lane, Dermot A. *Stepping Stones to Other Religions: A Christian Theology of Inter-religious Dialogue.* Dublin: Veritas, 2011.

Lefebure, Leo F. *True and Holy: Christian Scripture and Other Religions.* Maryknoll, NY: Orbis Books, 2013.

McDermott, Gerald, and Harold Netland, eds. *A Trinitarian Theology of Religions: An Evangelical Proposal.* New York: Oxford University Press, 2014.

Madigan, Daniel. *The Qur'an's Self-image: Writing and Authority in Islam's Scripture.* Princeton, NJ: Princeton University Press, 2001.

Merrigan, Terrence, and John Friday, eds. *The Past, Present, and Future of Theologies of Interreligious Dialogue.* Oxford: Oxford University Press, 2017.

Moreland, Anna Bonta. "The Qur'an and the Doctrine of Private Revelation: A Theological Proposal." *Theological Studies* 76 (2015): 531–49.

Moyaert, Maryanne, and Didier Pollefeyt, eds. *Never Revoked: Nostra Aetate as Ongoing Challenge for Jewish–Christian Dialogue.* Leuven: Peeters, 2010.

Nesbitt, Eleanor M. *Sikhism: A Very Short Introduction.* Oxford: Oxford University Press, 2005.

O'Collins, Gerald, and Michael A. Hayes, eds. *The Legacy of John Paul II.* London: Burns & Oates, 2008.

O'Connell, Gerard. *Do Not Stifle the Spirit: Conversations with Jacques Dupuis.* Maryknoll, NY: Orbis Books, 2017.

Panikkar, Raimundo. *The Unknown Christ of Hinduism: Towards an Ecumenical Christophany.* London: Darton, Longman & Todd, 1981.

————. *The Experience of God: Icons of the Mystery,* trans. Joseph Cunneen. Minneapolis, MN: Fortress Press, 2006.

Parrinder, Geoffrey. *Jesus in the Qur'an.* Oxford: Oneworld, 1995.

Phan, Peter C. *Being Religious Interreligiously: Asian Perspectives on Interfaith Dialogue.* Maryknoll, NY: Orbis Books, 2004.

————, ed. *Christianities in Asia.* Oxford: Wiley-Blackwell, 2011.

The Pontifical Biblical Commission, *The Jewish People and Their Sacred Scripture in the Christian Bible.* Vatican City: Libreria Editrice Vaticana, 2001.

Pratt, Douglas. *Being Open, Being Faithful: The Journey of Interreligious Dialogue.* Geneva: World Council of Churches, 2014.

Rahner, Karl. *Foundations of Christian Faith: An Introduction to the Idea of Christianity,* trans. William V. Dych, 138–75, 311–21. New York: Crossroad, 1978.

————. *Theological Investigations,* 23 vols. London: Darton, Longman & Todd, 1961–92. The theme of Christ/Christianity and "the others" recurs frequently, and is treated at chapter length in vols. 5, 6, 9, 12, 14, 16, 17, and 18.

Robinson, Neal. *Christ in Islam and Christianity: The Representation of Jesus in the Qur'an and the Classical Muslim Commentaries.* London: Macmillan, 1991.

Roggema, Barbara, et al., eds. *The Three Rings: Textual Studies in the Historical Trialogue of Judaism, Christianity and Islam.* Leuven: Peeters, 2005.

Ruokanen, Miikka. *The Catholic Doctrine on Non-Christian Religions According to the Second Vatican Council.* Leiden: Brill, 1992.

Ruthven, Malise. *Islam: A Very Short Introduction.* Oxford: Oxford University Press, 1997.

Schmidt-Leukel, Perry. *Gott ohne Grenzen: eine christliche und pluralistische Theologie der Religionen.* Gütersloh: Gütersloher Verlagshaus, 2008.

————. *Religious Pluralism and Interreligious Theology: The Gifford Lectures—An Extended Version.* Maryknoll, NY: Orbis Books, 2017.

Sharma, Arvind, and Katherine Young, eds. *Feminism and World Religions.* Albany: State University of New York, 1999.

Sherman, Franklin, ed. *Bridges: Documents of the Christian–Jewish Dialogue*, 2 vols. Mahwah, NJ: Paulist Press, 2011 and 2014.

Sherwin, Byron L., and Harold Kasimow, eds. *John Paul II and Interreligious Dialogue*. Maryknoll, NY: Orbis Books, 1999.

Siddiqui, Ataullah. *Christian–Muslim Dialogue in the Twentieth Century*. London: Macmillan, 1997.

Strange, David. *For Their Rock Is Not as Our Rock: An Evangelical Theology of Religions*. Leicester: Apollos, 2014.

Sullivan, Francis A. *Salvation Outside the Church? Tracing the History of the Catholic Response*. London: Geoffrey Chapman, 1992.

Volf, Miroslav. *Allah: A Christian Response*. New York: HarperOne, 2012.

Vorgrimler, Herbert, ed. *Commentary on the Documents of Vatican II*, 5 vols. London: Burns & Oates, 1967–69.

Waardenburg, Jean Jacques. *Muslims and Others; Relations in Context*. Berlin: Walter de Gruyter, 2003.

Ward, Veronica, and Richard Sherlock, eds. *Religion and Terrorism: The Use of Violence in Abrahamic Monotheism*. Lanham, MD: Rowman and Littlefield, 2014.

Wilfred, Felix, ed. *The Oxford Handbook of Christianity in Asia*. Oxford: Oxford University Press, 2014.

Gerald O'Collins on Christ and Other Religions

"Christ and Non-Christians." In Gerald O'Collins, *Fundamental Theology*, 114–29. New York: Paulist Press, 1981.

"Christ Beyond Christianity." In Gerald O'Collins, *Interpreting Jesus*, 202–8. London: Geoffrey Chapman, 1983.

"Saving Revelation for All People." In Gerald O'Collins, *Retrieving Fundamental Theology*, 79–86. Mahwah, NJ: Paulist Press, 1993.

"Universal Redeemer." In Gerald O'Collins, *Christology: A Biblical, Historical, and Systematic Study of Jesus*, 296–305. Oxford: Oxford University Press, 1995.

"Christ and the Religions." *Gregorianum* 84 (2003): 347–62.

"Jacques Dupuis's Contribution to Interreligious Dialogue." *Theological Studies* 64 (2003): 388–97.

Ed. (with Daniel Kendall). In Gerald O'Collins, *Many and Diverse Ways: In Honor of Jacques Dupuis*. Maryknoll, NY: Orbis Books, 2003.

"Jacques Dupuis: His Person and Work." In Gerald O'Collins, *Many and Diverse Ways: In Honor of Jacques Dupuis*, 18–29. Maryknoll, NY: Orbis Books, 2003.

"Jacques Dupuis, SJ (1923–2004): In Retrospect." *Vidyajvoti* 69 (2005): 450–59.

"Implementing *Nostra Aetate*." *Gregorianum* 87 (2006): 714–26.

"The Salvation of Non-Christians." In Gerald O'Collins, *Jesus Our Redeemer: A Christian Approach to Salvation*, 218–37. Oxford: Oxford University Press, 2007.

"John Paul II on Christ, the Holy Spirit, and World Religions." *Irish Theological Quarterly* 72 (2007): 323–37.

Salvation for All: God's Other Peoples. Oxford: Oxford University Press, 2008. *Horizons* 36 (2009) published a review symposium of this book that featured Francis X. Clooney, Catherine Cornille, Paul J. Griffiths, and Peter C. Phan (121–42).

"Universal Redeemer." In Gerald O'Collins, *Christology: A Biblical, Historical, and Systematic Study of Jesus*, 2nd ed., 315–33. Oxford: Oxford University Press, 2009.

"World Religions and Christ the Revealer and Saviour." In Gerald O'Collins, *Rethinking Fundamental Theology*, 292–321. Oxford: Oxford University Press, 2011.

"The Dupuis Case." In Gerald O'Collins, *On the Left Bank of the Tiber*, 213–51. Ballarat, AU: Connor Court, 2013.

"The Second Vatican Council and Other Living Faiths." *Pacifica* 26 (2013): 155–70.

The Second Vatican Council on Other Religions. Oxford: Oxford University Press, 2013.

"Jacques Dupuis: The Ongoing Debate." *Theological Studies* 74 (2013): 632–54. Reprinted as "Jacques Dupuis and Religious Pluralism." In Gerald O'Collins, *Christology: Origins, Developments, Debates*, 164–69, 209–29. Waco, TX: Baylor University Press, 2015.

"The Priesthood of Christ and the Followers of Other Living Faiths." *Irish Theological Quarterly* 78 (2013): 262–78. Reprinted in Gerald O'Collins, *Christology: Origins, Developments, Debates*, 89–107. Waco, TX: Baylor University Press, 2015.

"Was Jacques Dupuis a Neo-Rahnerian?" *Asian Horizons* 7 (2013): 237–60. Reprinted as "Jacques Dupuis and Karl Rahner." In Gerald O'Collins, *Christology: Origins, Developments, Debates*, 131–41, 169–72. Waco, TX: Baylor University Press, 2015.

"The Church and the Power of Prayer for 'the Others.'" *Horizons* 41 (2014): 211–29.

"The Theology of Religions Revisited." *Pacifica* 28 (2015): 54–67.

"The Faith of Others: A Biblical Possibility." *Irish Theological Quarterly* 80 (2015): 313–26.

"Vatican II on Other Ways of Salvation: A Valid Interpretation?" *Irish Theological Quarterly* 81 (2016): 152–70.

"The Divine Revelation Reaching the 'Others.'" In *Revelation: Towards a Christian Interpretation of God's Self-revelation in Jesus Christ,* 183–204. Oxford: Oxford University Press, 2016.

"Preface." In Gerard O'Connell, *Do Not Stifle the Spirit: Conversations with Jacques Dupuis,* ix–xi. Maryknoll, NY: Orbis Books, 2017.

"Vatican II on the Religions: A Response." *Nova et Vetera* 15 (2017): 1243–49.

Index of Biblical Passages

Index of Names